The Wiccan Book
of Rites and Rituals

Also by Sister Moon

○ ◑ ● ◐ ○

THE WICCANING
COLOR CASTING FOR WICCANS

The Wiccan Book of Rites and Rituals

○ ◑ ● ◐ ○

A Collection of Spells for Every Magickal Day of the Year

SISTER MOON

with the Coven of Witches and Legends

CITADEL PRESS
Kensington Publishing Corp.
www.kensingtonbooks.com

CITADEL PRESS books are published by

Kensington Publishing Corp.
850 Third Avenue
New York, NY 10022

All Kensington titles, imprints, and distributed lines are available at
special quantity discounts for bulk purchases for sales promotions,
premiums, fund-raising, educational, or institutional use. Special
book excerpts or customized printings can also be created to fit
specific needs. For details, write or phone the office of the Kensington special sales manager: Kensington Publishing Corp., 850 Third
Avenue, New York, NY 10022, attn: Special Sales Department;
phone 1-800-221-2647.

CITADEL PRESS and the Citadel Press logo
are Reg. U.S. Pat. and TM Off.

Interior design by Rachel Reiss

First printing: June 2004
10 9 8 7 6 5 4 3 2 1
Printed in the United States of America

Library of Congress Control Number: 2003112329

ISBN 0-8065-2535-5

This book has two dedications:
the first, to the Goddess, with all
of our love, energy, devotion, and
passion; and the second, to all of
those individuals who are inspired
daily to worship the Goddess,
dance naked in the moonlight, and
join hands in celebration of our
Wiccan heritage.

Contents

• To cleanse the energies in a bedroom • A ritual of
thanksgiving • A ritual to honor Crones and Wizards
• For truth to be told in legal matters

Preface

This book is bound by magick. The words of printed ink are the tears and blood of each Witch who touched it and cast the spells. Passing through the ages, it gains a more significant power than when it originated. Ageless, the magick within these pages will survive the duration of time. Each Witch who casts spells from within this book will eternally feel the connection of Goddess, God, love, sisterhood, brotherhood, and the never-waning power of the Moon.

The products listed in this book are everyday products that you will find at your local neighborhood occult store. Some of them may have somewhat different names in your locale. If you can't find something called for in these spells, ask a Wiccan practitioner or occult store owner what the alternate name may be so you will be assured of using the right product. There are a number of on-line occult stores that carry many of these products and will be able to assist you. If all else fails, write to Mountain Gypsies, P.O. Box 2995, Loveland, Colorado 80539, or call 970-667-3772 and place your order. This supplier carries all incenses, oils, and bath salts called for in these pages.

In Wicca, we have the rule of three: Whatever harm is done to others will come back to the caster threefold. I also believe in the opposite: Whatever good you do will come back to you threefold.

When preparing to cast magick, remember not to take every piece of an herb but, rather, leave some behind so that it may continue to grow. The man in the following poem forgot this rule. He wanted everything that he could get for himself, but he forgot to give back for all that he took. In doing this, he was harming his spirit in ways that he didn't understand until it was too late. So please, if you decide to cast a spell or simply perform a ritual, remember to "Always Give Back" in one way or another.

Always Give Back

My desire was to find a book to read,
But not the same topic, my friend indeed,
As often as I have read before;
This book I wanted was hidden lore.

Late one night looking o'er many a tome,
I found a book: of gold it shone.
The title was worn, the pages brittle.
My heart, the traitor, it skipped a little.

The first page I came to was weathered brown.
All I could think was, "What's this I've found?"
Upon reading its writ, I couldn't turn back—
"Heed ye this: Take care to always give back."

Greedily I thirsted and hungered for more;
I grabbed this volume and flew to the door.
Looking back, you would have to agree
This book of spells was not for me.

Page after page, I read with glee,
This out of my hands never to let be.
Rites, Incants, Songs I would sing,
Spells I cast till my ears did ring.

I gathered materials, from whence I didn't care,
To bring me my dreams and make them my fair.
I never thought to replace a thing:
Everything was mine, all there for the taking.

Gaunt, shriveled, inside a healthy host,
A drink of life my soul wanted most.
The warning unheeding when first off the shelf,
How was I to know I was hurting myself?

Now as I lay here, broken and torn,
Not in body, but in spirit alone.
One thought in my mind keeps coming back,
"Take care, take care to always give back."

—The Knight in Shining Amour,
an American Soldier/Warlock

Acknowledgments

We wish to express our undying gratitude to our significant life partners, family members, children, mentors, and friends for making this book possible. To each and every Witch and Warlock that contributed their spells and magick. A special thanks to Matt, Andy, Kevin, Lindsey, Jay, Scott, John, Bear, Michael, Robin, and Steve for your patience and support during this process. To Margaret Wolf at Citadel Press for her all-knowing wisdom in the arrangement of spells.

Table of Magickal Hours of the Day

HOURS

A.M.	SUN.	MON.	TUES.	WED.	THURS.	FRI.	SAT.
1:00	Sun	Moon	Mars	Merc.	Jup.	Ven.	Sat.
2:00	Ven.	Sat.	Sun	Moon	Mars	Merc.	Jup.
3:00	Merc.	Jup.	Ven.	Sat.	Sun	Moon	Mars
4:00	Moon	Mars	Merc.	Jup.	Ven.	Sat.	Sun
5:00	Sat.	Sun	Moon	Mars	Merc.	Jup.	Ven.
6:00	Jup.	Ven.	Sat.	Sun	Moon	Mars	Merc.
7:00	Mars	Merc.	Jup.	Ven.	Sat.	Sun	Moon
8:00	Sun	Moon	Mars	Merc.	Jup.	Ven.	Sat.
9:00	Ven.	Sat.	Sun	Moon	Mars	Merc.	Jup.
10:00	Merc.	Jup.	Ven.	Sat.	Sun	Moon	Mars
11:00	Moon	Mars	Merc.	Jup.	Ven.	Sat.	Sun.
12:00	Sat.	Sun	Moon	Mars	Merc.	Jup.	Ven.

Table of Magickal Hours of the Night

A.M.	SUN.	MON.	TUES.	WED.	THURS.	FRI.	SAT.
1:00	Jup.	Ven.	Sat.	Sun	Moon	Mars	Merc.
2:00	Mars	Merc.	Jup.	Ven.	Sat.	Sun	Moon
3:00	Sun	Moon	Mars	Merc.	Jup.	Ven.	Sat.
4:00	Ven.	Sat.	Sun	Moon	Mars	Merc.	Jup.
5:00	Merc.	Jup.	Ven.	Sat.	Sun	Moon	Mars
6:00	Moon	Mars	Merc.	Jup.	Ven.	Sat.	Sun
7:00	Sat.	Sun	Moon	Mars	Merc.	Jup.	Ven.
8:00	Jup.	Ven.	Sat.	Sun	Moon	Mars	Merc.
9:00	Mars	Merc.	Jup.	Ven.	Sat.	Sun	Moon
10:00	Sun	Moon	Mars	Merc.	Jup.	Ven.	Sat.
11:00	Ven.	Sat.	Sun	Moon	Mars	Merc.	Jup.
12:00	Merc.	Jup.	Ven.	Sat.	Sun	Moon	Mars

The Wiccan Book
of Rites and Rituals

ONE

The Wolf's Moon

The mountain canyon echoes the howl,
Of the lonely wolf on the prowl.
It's gentle, sweet music to the Witch's ear,
And comforts the soul to know wolves near.

The Wolf's Moon in January is the time to perform rituals dealing with independence, good fortune, the first chakra, natural instincts, wisdom, protection in every aspect, home and family, animals in the wild, healing the Earth, healing in general, aiding the needy, divining future partners, and happiness. It is also the time for rituals that honor the Goddess. This is also a time to banish idleness, stagnation, indecision, and loneliness. While the Full Moon is the most powerful time for spell casting, the Hare Moon (the New Moon) is the next best time and can be considered a substitute.

The Witch Who Cried "Wolf"

A Solitary Ritual (Yellow)
by Sister Moon

MAGICKAL INTENTION: To dispel loneliness.

TIME: Wolf's Moon, Sun hour

TOOLS: Three yellow candles, High Meadows oil, Wolf's Song incense, a very small tuft of wolf's bane,* glue, wind chimes, and a small mirror.

INSTRUCTIONS: Anoint the candles with High Meadows oil. Place the candles in a triangle. Light the candles and the incense. Attach the tuft of wolf's bane to the chime using a dab of glue. Attach the small mirror to the wind chimes. Anoint the chimes with the oil. Pass the chimes and mirror through the incense smoke thirteen times deosil (clockwise) while reciting the incantation.

Hang the wind chimes near a window outside of your bedroom area. Each time the chimes sound, your spell is put out into the universe. The mirror will signal with a reflection on your walls each time it sends you a decent friend. Keep an open heart and an open eye when addressing new people. Be prepared to share good times and good friendships.

---

* In most places, wolf's bane (a tuft of wolf's fur, not to be confused with wolfs-bane, which is a plant) is difficult to come by. You can obtain a small tuft of it by submitting your request, a self-addressed, stamped envelope, and a donation to: Rocky Mountain Wolf Rescue, P.O. Box 1544, LaPorte, CO 80535

INCANTATION:

> The lonely Witch draws moonlight,
> Calling the Children of the Night.
> Musical chimes will reach their ears,
> Of lonely wolves drawing near.
> The magickal tune will sing with delight,
> And reflect a signal with dancing light.
> Each time a wolf will make a friend,
> And put this loneliness to an end.
> So Mote It Be.

○ ◐ ● ◑ ○

Bringing in the Power

Coven Ritual (Purple)
by Whilterna

MAGICKAL INTENTION: A ritual to honor the Goddess and to restore a Witch's power.

TIME: Full Moon or Hare Moon in January, Moon hour

TOOLS: A fully set altar of tools, one purple candle, one white candle, King Solomon oil, Wolf's Song incense, Goddess oil, a red flannel mojo, an aquamarine, a bloodstone, a piece of malachite, a pinch of each of the following: kelp, mint, celery, cotton, cedar, corn, sage, sweetgrass, sandalwood, jasmine, and frankincense; and a crystal bell.

INSTRUCTIONS: This is a full ritual. Begin with the full call of order including sweeping the circle. Anoint the purple and white candles with the King Solomon oil. Light the candles and the incense. As the High Priestess recites "The Beginnings" (below), each participant places one of the ingredients (aquamarine through frankincense) into the mojo.

When all of the ingredients have been added, the High Priestess passes the mojo through the incense smoke and adds three drops of Goddess and King Solomon oils to it. She then recites the incantation and rings the bell. Pass the mojo around the circle so each member can receive its power.

The mojo can be passed through the smoke of Wolf's Song incense anytime the coven members need to reenergize their power.

THE BEGINNINGS:
> The Circle is cast.
> The Watch Towers are set.
> The Guardians are here; and
> The Powers That Be attend and assist.
> In the making,
> Draw in some Power.
> Infuse the Light into these works.
> Each step is a process precise,
> To bring in power right.
> Whether it be Dark of the Moon, or Full of the Moon,
> Sunrise or Sunset,
> Pure Light of High Power to my life, love, and works,
>   will attend.
> Draw the power within.
> Drink of its full flavor.
> Savor the body while filling with bright, white light.
> Pass the amulet through the smoke of High Power.

Do this to make it yours, not ours.
Pass it again, a time of your choosing.
Do this for strength renewing.
And So It Is and So Mote It Be.

THE INCANTATION:
Take a pouch that is bright and gay,
Add to it stones of power, love, discernment.
A stone of amplification and penetration, an ultimate
    goal,
A truth star which comes from a diamond bright and
    rare.
A stone of very great power is the bloodstone.
For growth and discernment, malachite will be on
    hand.
Psychic power from the sea's own life,
The herb of kelp, water delight.
Blend together Fire and Air.
Light will burst from the pair.
On the Air is the smell of mint,
While Fire might, celery will produce.
Add from Earth, a wick to sustain the light.
Threads of cotton, the trick will do.
Now for Wisdom and Protection,
Add cedar, corn, and sage.
Add a pinch of sweetgrass for pure intent.
Drops of Mystic Gift and pinch of sandalwood
For psychic development and growth.
Jasmine to heighten the power.
Frankincense we add for protection.
And oil of wisdom to use the power well.
Ring three times the bell.

Once for the child, once for the maid, and once for
the crone.
So Mote It Be.

○ ◐ ● ◑ ○

A Helping Hand

Solitary or Coven Ritual (Green)
by Nova

MAGICKAL INTENTION: To help the less fortunate and promote generosity.

TIME: Full Moon in January, Jupiter hour

TOOLS: One green candle, Helping Hand oil, Jade incense, a pot with a circumference of at least ten inches, potting soil, and three small aloe plants.

INSTRUCTIONS: Anoint the candle with the Helping Hand oil, and light the candle and the incense. Visualize the wealthy becoming more generous and spreading their prosperity among less-fortunate people. Pot each aloe plant, reciting the incantation for each one. As the plants grow, so will the aid to the needy.

INCANTATION:
As these healing aloe plants grow,
Let the less fortunates' plight show.
As the plant increase in the sun's light,
And continually grow to a great height.
Let generosity widely spread,

And the pressures on those in need be shed.
Generous people of stature and wealth,
Aid the needy in life and in health.
So Mote It Be.

○ ◐ ● ◑ ○

A Potion of Peace

Solitary or Coven Ritual (Brown)
by Queen of the Meadow

MAGICKAL INTENTION: To make a home peaceful.

TIME: Full Moon or Hare Moon in January, Sun hour

TOOLS: One brown candle, Peace oil, Ravenwood incense, small pinches of rosemary, mint, dill, and carnation, one quart of water, an earthen pot, and one dark brown bottle.

INSTRUCTIONS: Anoint the candle with the Peace oil. Light the candle and the incense. Place the water and the herbs into the earthen pot and allow to boil for exactly seven minutes. Remove the infusion from the heat and pour it into the dark brown bottle. Leave the bottle on a windowsill so the Full Moon shines upon it and energizes it. Recite the incantation. Sprinkle the infusion in every corner of every room of the home. The home will have calmer, more peaceful energy instantly.

INCANTATION:
I conjure this power of tranquil peace,
Make all trouble disperse and decease.

Encompass our home as a united nation,
Rosemary, mint, dill, and carnation.
I conjure this power that I infuse,
With peaceful energy that cannot refuse.
I conjure this power of the wolf and raven,
To make our home a more peaceful haven.
So Mote It Be.

○ ◑ ● ◐ ○

Brave Heart

Solitary Ritual (Red)
by Sister Moon

MAGICKAL INTENTION: To create an amulet that provides the ability to be confident, independent, and strong in times of struggle.

TIME: Full Moon in January, Mars hour

TOOLS: One red candle, Mandrake oil, Wolf's Song incense, three pinches of St. John's wort, one garnet, and one red flannel mojo.

INSTRUCTIONS: Anoint the candle with Mandrake oil. Light the candle and the incense. Place the St. John's wort and the garnet into the red mojo and tie it shut. Working deosil, pass the mojo through the incense smoke three times. Recite the incantation. Place the mojo over your heart and keep it with you any time you feel weak.

INCANTATION:

> Over my heart, I conquer the dark.
> Upon my breast, I feel my quest.
> With this stone, I'm comfortable alone.
> No weakness or wave, for I am brave.
> So Mote It Be.

○ ◑ ● ◑ ○

Protected Places

Solitary Ritual (Blue)
by Raiya

MAGICKAL INTENTION: To protect a house from negativity.

TIME: Full Moon in January, Mars hour

TOOLS: Four small blue candles, Lotus oil, Tranquillity and House Blessing incenses, a cauldron, and a pinch each of basil, wisteria, lavender, and clove.

INSTRUCTIONS: Anoint the four candles with the Lotus oil. Light the candles and place them in north, south, east, and west corners of the home. Combine the herbs with the two incenses in the cauldron and light them. Fumigate each room of the house with the incense smoke while reciting the incantation. Light the candles whenever you feel the need to boost the protection.

INCANTATION:

> Goddess protect this home and hearth,
> Bring positive energy from our Earth.

Protect this house from evil and sadness,
Do away with corruption and madness.
Banish the danger and the toil,
Draw the positive to our soil.
Only love and happiness will fill this home,
Protect this place I call my own.
So Mote It Be.

○ ◐ ● ◑ ○

Talisman of Wisdom

Solitary or Coven Ritual (Dark Green/Black)
by Whilterna

MAGICKAL INTENTION: To create a talisman that inspires deep knowledge.

TIME: Full Moon in January or any Blue Moon, Mercury hour

TOOLS: One dark green candle to represent deep knowledge, one black candle to represent mysteries, Frankincense oil, sage incense, emerald, citron, jasper, and quartz stones, herbs of sage, sunflower, savory and caraway, one three-inch square of dark green felt, one four-inch square of black felt, and a nine-inch piece of gold string or ribbon.

INSTRUCTIONS: Anoint the candles with the Frankincense oil. Light the candles and the incense. Place the green candle on the right of the altar and the black candle on the left of the altar. Place the herbs and the stones in the center of the dark green felt square.

Place the dark green square on top of the black square and pull the points together at the center, creating a bag. Tie the gold string three times around the mouth of the bag and knot it.

Anoint the talisman thrice around the triple-triple. Recite the incantation, pass the talisman through the incense smoke in deosil motion three times.

When you desire the answer to a question be revealed, swing the talisman from right to left and then hold it to your heart. Ask your question. Place talisman on your third eye. Then swing the talisman from left to right and say the words, "Blessed Be, Blessed Be." The answer will be revealed within a short time.

INCANTATION:
On Nature's Way, let the talisman lay.
Take the candle in hand each in its turn.
Deep knowledge first then the Mysteries at hand.
Anoint to the Sun from Earth do now.
And honor the Triple–Triple.
Then again back thrice do you go.
Set their bases in holders well.
Deep Knowledge on the right.
And the Mysteries on the left.
Bring Fire to bear on Wisdom and Balance.
Through the smoke goes the talisman.
For the directions, Above and Below,
Do not forget the Spirit also.
Seven times says it all.
Ask what you will for Deep Knowledge and Mysteries.
But first you must bright light to darkness.
Passing right to left,
Then ask what may with talisman to heart.
Place talisman to mind's eye at end of request.

It is good, So Mote It Be.
Now bring darkness to light.
From left to right.
Speak, "Blessed Be" and "Blessed Be."
This is done on High Full Moon.
Be it Wolf or be it Blue.
It is done!
So Mote It Be.

TWO

Candlemas

Eight colored candles all aglow,
On Candlemas Eve, a Witch will know.
To conjure a rainbow of magick and sun,
To warm the earth when winter is done.

Candlemas is on February 1 or 2, and it is a major Sabbat for Wiccans. This is the time to perform rituals to get rid of old and unwanted energy, to bring in new and positive energy, to banish darkness from your life, and for any ritual regarding traditions, rainbows, fertility, color magick, hope, missions, special care to animals, preparation of seeds, weavings, quilts, wishing wells, cloaks, capes, and protection.

The Fertile Body

Solitary Ritual (Rainbow magick with emphasis of Green)
by Aquila Eagle

MAGICKAL INTENTION: To help the body to become more fertile.

TIME: February 1 or 2, Waxing or Waning Moon, Sun hour. This ritual is to be repeated each night for seven nights.

TOOLS: A lavender and white altar cloth; Fertility oil; one large green candle; one votive candle in each of the following colors: yellow, orange, red, blue and purple; Blessed Be incense; two tablespoons each of ginseng, acorn, olive, and sunflower; a mortar and pestle; and seven red flannel mojo bags.

INSTRUCTIONS: Place the altar cloth on your clean altar before you begin. Anoint the green candle in Fertility oil. Place the votive candles around the green candle. Place the incense to the left of the candles and light the incense and the candles. Place a pinch of each herb into the mortar and pestle and crush them. Add six drops of Fertility oil and grind them once again. Recite the incantation over the mixture. Place the mixture in one of the red flannel bags and pass it in deosil motion through the incense smoke three times. Recite the incantation again.

Keep each mojo beneath your bed until the seventh mojo is done. Take your seven mojos to where there is an abundance of clover and bury them there. Recite the incantation once again.

INCANTATION:

> Body and soul open up and cleanse,
> Fill with purity, love, and happiness.
> Protect and calm emotions around,

So that a fertile environment is abound.
My wish is for fertility,
With ultimate dreams of being a good
parent unconditionally.
So Mote It Be.

○ ◑ ● ◐ ○

Night Mares

Solitary or Coven Ritual (Yellow)
by Colleechee

MAGICKAL INTENTION: To bless the horses that are preparing to give birth in the spring. This ritual aids the mare in delivery and blesses the colts with good health and a free spirit.

TIME: February 1 or 2, Midnight hour

TOOLS: One yellow candle, Good Health oil, Springtime incense, a 13-inch-by-13-inch piece of yellow cloth, yellow thread, one hair carefully cut from the mare's tail, a pinch each of coltsfoot, horseradish, black cohosh, and primrose, a sprig of eucalyptus, and a straw from a Witch's broom.

INSTRUCTIONS: Anoint the candle with the oil. Light the candle and the incense. Make a bag out of the yellow cloth and sew it with the yellow thread. Place all of the ingredients (the hair through the broom straw) into the bag, and sew it shut. Anoint the bag with the oil. Pass the bag in deosil motion through the incense smoke thirteen times while reciting the incantation.

Keep the bag in the dark until the mare is in labor, then place the bag beneath her to ensure a safe and easy delivery of the colt. When the colt is born, bury the bag with the placenta.

INCANTATION:

> Within this pouch of golden sun,
> I summon the power of the painless
>   one.
> Ease the labor of expectant horse,
> Make this birth an easy course.
> Painless is the magickal key,
> Short and fast is the delivery.
> Birth the colt good health and fair,
> And gain the magick of the Night Mare.
> So Mote It Be.

Rays of Power

Solitary or Coven Ritual (Purple)
by Lyra

MAGICKAL INTENTION: To burn out the darkness with the power of the sun.

TIME: February 1 or 2, Sunrise hour

TOOLS: A cauldron, one purple candle, one white candle, Witch oil, New Life incense, and amaranth, cypress, morning glory, Solomon's seal, and tamarisk herbs.

INSTRUCTIONS: Face east just before the sunrise and create a small bonfire in the cauldron. Anoint the two candles with the oil. Just as the sun begins to rise, sprinkle the incense into the fire. Light the candles, and toss the herbs into the fire. Stand with your arms raised to the sun and recite the incantation. When the fire has burned out completely, bury the ashes in the earth.

INCANTATION:

> The fiery gold orb will soon arise,
> To burn away the dark of night.
> To purify the world and light the skies,
> Cleanse all souls and make things right.
> Power is ours to replenish our spirits,
> Draw the veil from our eyes.
> Give us life with the Sun,
> The banishment of darkness has now begun.
> So Mote It Be.

○ ◐ ● ◑ ○

Negative No More

Coven Ritual (White/Purple)
by Willow

MAGICKAL INTENTION: To banish negative and stagnant energy.

TIME: February 1 or 2, Saturn hour

TOOLS: One large white candle, Rose Cross oil and incense, thirty-two ounces of 7-Up, the juice of one coconut, the juice of one lemon, thirteen smashed grapes, seven drops of peppermint oil, a large pitcher, one yucca leaf, a chalice for each participant, a white mojo, a small piece of coconut shell, one grape seed, three small slices of lemon rind, several grape stems, a dash of peppermint extract, and one banded amethyst stone.

INSTRUCTIONS: Anoint the candle with the Rose Cross oil. Light the candle and the incense. Combine the next five ingredients (7-Up through peppermint) in the pitcher and stir the brew in deosil motion seven times with the yucca leaf. Pour the mixture into the chalices while visualizing the negative energy that you would like to be rid of. Recite Incantation One, and drink the brew.

Next, place the next six ingredients (coconut shell through amethyst) in the mojo and anoint the mojo with the oil. Feel pure, white, positive energy moving into your body and soul. Each participant should pass the mojo in deosil motion through the incense smoke three times. Place the mojo in the center of the circle. All participants should link hands and recite Incantation Two.

INCANTATION ONE:

> Gathered here on Candlemas night,
> To chase away our negative plight.
> Five flavors in the Witches brew,
> Combined to bring something new.
> A little taste of sweet and sour,
> Makes the old have no power.
> With the stir of a yucca twig,
> So goes away the negative.
> Start the waters of life flowing,
> Keep the good and new a-growing.
> Drink with Coven to set in motion,
> The positive energy of this potion.
> So Mote It Be.

INCANTATION TWO:

> One grape seed and coconut skin,
> Banish negative energy that lingers within.
> Add some purifying stones with the sour rind,
> Only positive energies fill out body and mind.
> So Mote It Be.

○ ◐ ● ◑ ○

The Tattered Cloak

Coven Ritual (Rainbow Magick with emphasis on purple)
by Sister Moon

MAGICKAL INTENTION: To empower a cape or cloak with magick and power.

TIME: February 1 or 2, any hour

TOOLS: One purple candle, Wicca oil, Witch incense, thirteen magickal stones of your choosing, an old or new cape, and needles and thread.

INSTRUCTIONS: This is the time to repair any cape you already have or make a special member a new cape and empower it.

Assemble a full Coven with a full Call of Order. Anoint the candle with the oil. Light the candle and the incense. Place the stones in the center of the circle. The High Priestess will anoint them and recite the Incantation. Place the stones in the hem of the cape and hand-stitch them in. (After the ritual is over, you can machine-sew the hem to strengthen the stitches.) The Coven links hands with the High Priestess in the center of the circle. Pass the cape through the incense smoke, and perform the call and response (below).

INCANTATION ONE:

> Around the moon and around the sun,
> Empower these stones gathered as one.
> Release your magick as we invoke,
> All the power within this cloak.
> So Mote It Be.

CALL AND RESPONSE:

> HIGH PRIESTESS:
>> Precious stones and precious gems,
>> Secretly gathered within the hem.
>
> PARTICIPANTS:
>> Power within the circle round,
>> Bridled energy draws the moon down.
>
> HIGH PRIESTESS:
>> Wearer and bearer of this cape,
>> From head to toe it shall drape.
>
> PARTICIPANTS:
>> Power within the circle round,
>> Bridled energy draws the moon down.
>
> HIGH PRIESTESS:
>> Empower this Witch wearer of this cloak,
>> Unleash her powers within this smoke.
>
> PARTICIPANTS:
>> Power within the circle round,
>> Bridled energy draws the moon down.
>
> HIGH PRIESTESS:
>> So Mote It Be.

PARTICIPANTS:
> So Mote It Be.
> So Mote It Be.
> So Mote It Be!

○ ◐ ● ◑ ○

Well of Tears

Coven or Solitary Ritual (Purple)
by Sister Moon

MAGICKAL INTENTION: To replenish the magick of a wishing well.

TIME: February 1 or 2, Moon hour

TOOLS: One purple candle, Magick oil, Witching Well incense, and a collection of tears from a Witch or Witches. (Tears can be collected in vials for this ritual.)

INSTRUCTIONS: Take the candle, the oil, the incense, and the tears to a wishing well at the Moon hour on Candlemas. Anoint the candle with the oil. Light the candle and the incense. Apply the Magick oil to all of your pulse points. Recite the incantation and add the tears into the well. This will activate the magick of the well for one full year. If the well has been dry of Witches' tears for many years, a full coven must assemble and add their tears to replenish the magick of the well.

INCANTATION:

Deep within the wishing wells,
Conjure the magick, wishes, and spells.
Always giving the caster hope,
Sharing in dreams and ways to cope.
On Candlemas day, the well has dried,
'Til the Witch deposits tears she cried.
Replenish the wells so hollow and tragic,
Recite these words to awaken the magick.
"Candlemas well, wishes and dreams,
Conjure mirror and earthly streams.
Carry these tears to the winter faeries,
To fulfill the wishes that are legendary."
The spell is cast and the well is alive!
Candlemas magick will certainly thrive!
For one full year, this magick and spell,
Satisfies the dreams of the wishing well.
So Mote It Be.

THREE

The Storm Moon

Thunder and lightning in the night,
A Witch's broom soon takes flight.
Casting a blanket to shelter from storm,
That goodness welcomes and evil scorns.

The Full Moon in February is known as The Storm Moon. This is a time to perform rituals dealing with communications, personal wealth, strengthening and healing the mind and memory, purity of heart, assistance in legal battles, preparation for any battle, healings, cleansing of the body and the spirit, family harmony, promoting areas of attraction, rededication of life and soul purpose, and for strengthening all relationships of importance. It is also time for protection from poverty, protection for all loved ones, protection from severe weather, protection for travelers, and protection for animals in general.

Under My Umbrella

Solitary or Coven Ritual (Blue)
by Crystal Ball

MAGICKAL INTENTION: For protection of all domestic animals.

TIME: Full Moon in February, Sun hour

TOOLS: One blue candle, Lotus oil, Protection incense, a small paper umbrella (like the kind that garnishes tropical cocktails), and a St. Francis medallion.

INSTRUCTIONS: Anoint the candle with the oil. Light the candle and the incense. Dig a hole in your backyard. Place the St. Francis medallion into the hole and bury it. Place the umbrella over it and recite the incantation. Leave the umbrella in there until it naturally blows away. It will keep your pet safe for a whole year.

INCANTATION:

> We don't mean to cause alarm,
> Just keep our pets safe from harm.
> The saint will bless,
> All animals and pets.
> From every wind and storm,
> The animals will be warned.
> The umbrella will protect,
> From hate and neglect.
> It shelters the young and old,
> And all creatures from cold.
> Safe and sound the animals will be.
> This is my will, So Mote It Be.

○ ◐ ● ◑ ○

The Midas Touch

Solitary or Coven Ritual (Green/Gold)
by Ariel

MAGICKAL INTENTION: To increase personal wealth.

TIME: Full Moon in February, Jupiter hour

TOOLS: One green candle, one gold candle, one orange candle, Midas oil, Golden Emerald incense, a citrine, a Sun stone, a green tourmaline, and one small red mojo.

INSTRUCTIONS: Anoint all three candles with Midas oil. Light the candles and the incense. Anoint each stone with the oil, place in the mojo, and tie it shut. Recite the incantation while passing the mojo in deosil motion ten times through the incense smoke. Bury the mojo by the light of the full moon. To keep the spell active, every three months anoint the ground covering the mojo with three drops of Midas oil while reciting the incantation.

INCANTATION:

> For the wealth we have,
> And the wealth to come.
> Grant me this wisdom,
> To guard it well.
> Protect us always,
> From those who dare.
> To take all we have,
> Without a care.

Great Goddess please,
Hear and answer my prayer.
So Mote It Be.

○ ◐ ● ◑ ○

The Friendship Quilt

Coven Ritual (Blue)
by Sister Moon

MAGICKAL INTENTION: To blanket our friends, our animals, and our loved ones from harm and to keep them safe.

TIME: Full Moon in February, Sun hour

TOOLS: This project is to create a patchwork quilt. Assemble a blue candle for each participant, Witching Well oil, Protection incense, a needle and white thread for each participant, and approximately four hundred three-inch-by-four-inch squares of fabric (blue cotton material will work best).

INSTRUCTIONS: Anoint all of the blue candles with Witching Well oil. Light the candles and the incense. Cast a circle and make sure that everyone is comfortable, because this spell will take a couple of hours. Each Witch is to be responsible for bringing her or his share of the fabric.

Begin by sewing four squares of fabric together to create a larger square. Do this until all of the small squares are used. As you are sewing the squares, make sure your stitches are close together and secure. Visualize these squares becoming a veil of protection for those in need.

Pass the completed squares through the incense smoke. Now sew together all of the large squares until all of the pieces make one large blanket. Recite the incantation. Anoint the corners of the quilt and open the circle.

It is traditional for the Coven to give this blanket to any member who is in need of protection for their household. The Coven can also keep the blanket and use it for summer festivals to picnic upon.

INCANTATION:

> Friends from far and friends so near,
> Friends we touch and friends we hear.
> Gather beneath the blanketed spell,
> For safety and protection where you dwell.
> The rounded moon will hear our plea,
> And energies of blue will encompass thee.
> Witch to Witch, friend to friend,
> Warmth and love is what we send.
> Mile to mile, sea to sea,
> The Friendship Quilt covers thee.
> Stitch to stitch, thread to thread,
> Protection is woven around your bed.
> Better your world, better your year,
> No longer hunger or know of fear.
> The earth will mend stitch by stitch,
> Woven in love by hands of the Witch.
> So Mote It Be.

○ ◑ ● ◐ ○

Whirly Winds

Solitary Ritual (Pink)
by Astra

MAGICKAL INTENTION: To increase communication within a relationship.

TIME: Full Moon in February, Moon hour

TOOLS: One pink candle, Sweetheart oil, a small cauldron, three strands of hair from each person, three nail clippings from both people, and three pinches each of catnip, copal, iris, morning glory, sage, savory, slippery elm, walnut, and yew.

INSTRUCTIONS: Anoint the candle with the oil. Light the candle. Place the hair, nail clippings, and herbs in the cauldron and mix them together. Recite the incantation three times, each time adding three drops of oil on the mixture (nine drops in all).

Place the cauldron outside in a safe place where it can be left for a while, and let the wind do the rest! Do not bring the cauldron back into the house until all of the mixture has blown away.

INCANTATION:

> With these locks of love and nails of stability,
> Invoke the magickal herbs with all ability.
> The powers of the Storm Moon grow,
> As the gentle wind may blow.
> Communication becomes stronger,
> As relationships of love begin to conquer.
> Let nature take her course,
> Using her powerful wind with force.
> So Mote It Be.

○ ◐ ● ◐ ○

Aphrodite's Allure

Solitary Ritual (Orange)
by Rising Star

MAGICKAL INTENTION: To attract anyone or anything you desire.

TIME: Hare Moon in February, Mars hour

TOOLS: One orange candle, Aphrodite oil and incense, a black cape, a picture of the person or object that you desire to attract, and a red flannel mojo.

INSTRUCTIONS: Anoint the candle with the oil and light the candle and the incense. Put on the cape. Place the picture inside the red mojo and seal it. Anoint the mojo with the Aphrodite oil and pass it through the incense smoke.

Find a fertile garden or field and bury the mojo in the earth. If there is snow on the ground, bury it in the snow. Stand over the buried mojo and turn in deosil motion three time; recite the incantation.

Leave the area but mark it—come back to the area on the full moon in the hour of Venus, and retrieve the mojo. Keep the mojo with you until you achieve what you desired. When you have, bury the mojo deep in the earth.

INCANTATION:

> Place the cape about thy wear,
> When attraction is the focused fare.
> Within the garden of winter's snow,

The maiden will come with desire to sow.
Aphrodite, I call your name,
Attraction is what I seek to gain.
Buried deep in the blanket of white,
And turned three times in deosil tight.
Retrieve this sack of crimson wool,
Upon the night the moon is full.
So Mote It Be.

○ ◑ ● ◐ ○

Healing Brew

Solitary Ritual (Yellow)
by Sister Moon

MAGICKAL INTENTION: Healing remedy for a lingering cold or virus.

TIME: Hare Moon in February, sunrise and sunset

TOOLS: One small package of chicken legs and thighs (with skin), a quarter cup of chopped onions, three quarts of water, a large pot, a crock pot, three tablespoons of echinacea, three tablespoons of garlic powder, one teaspoon of black pepper, three tablespoons of goldenseal, one tablespoon of onion salt, a pinch of basil, a pinch of ground ginger, thirteen cubes of chicken bouillion, one heaping tablespoon of chicken soup starter, one half cup of chopped carrots, one half cup of fresh peas, one and a half cups of pinwheel-shaped noodles, five tablespoons of healing bath salts, one yellow candle, Sunshine oil, and Healing incense.

INSTRUCTIONS: At sunrise, add the chicken and chopped onions to the water in a large pot. Let simmer for one hour. Recite the incantation over the brew.

Allow the brew to cool; skim the fat and skin from the liquid; remove the chicken and tear it into small chunks.

Place the chicken and the broth into a crock pot and set on low or medium heat. Add all the next nine ingredients (echinacea through soup starter) to the brew and recite the incantation. Allow the brew to cook for three and one half hours.

Add the carrots and peas to the brew and allow to cook for three more hours. Recite the incantation, add the pinwheel noodles, and cook for one hour.

Recite the incantation, turn off the crock pot, and allow the brew to sit for a minimum of three hours.

After sunset, reheat the brew.

Draw a hot bath and add the healing bath salts. Anoint the candle with the oil and light the candle and the incense in the room with the bath. Recite the incantation one final time over the bathwater. Turn off the lights, get in the bath, and eat the brew by the light of the candle. Relax.

You will need to eat the brew for three consecutive days, drink plenty of clear fluids, and rest. Allow your body the time to heal. Before the moon is full, healing will occur.

INCANTATION:
> Sanction this brew of double power,
> Herbs, spices and healing flowers.
> Moon be absent while potion sparks,
> Releasing the cure when drunk in the dark.
> So Mote It Be.

○ ◐ ● ◑ ○

The Goddess of Love

Solitary Ritual (Pink)
by Journey

MAGICKAL INTENTION: To experience the unconditional love of the Goddess.

TIME: Full Moon in February, Venus hour

TOOLS: One white candle, Goddess oil, Venus incense, a pink cloth approximately three and a half feet long and two feet wide (like a bath towel), and one sheet of white paper that is folded into a fan.

INSTRUCTIONS: This ritual is best performed skyclad, outdoors if possible. Feel the power of the Full Moon bathe your entire body. Anoint the candle with the Goddess oil. Light the candle and the incense. Place the pink cloth on the ground in front of the altar. Sit on the cloth and recite the incantation. Use the paper fan to waft incense smoke in deosil motion over your entire body. Allow the time to feel the presence of the Goddess and absorb the complete purity and acceptance of Her love.

INCANTATION:
>I call upon the Goddess to be with me,
>Clear my heart and mind so that I may see.
>I ask Goddess to be in Your presence,
>Let my body absorb Your essence.
>Guide my path with love on this Storm Moon night,
>Give me help with all Your might.
>I honor Your Moon shining above,
>Light and fill me with your love.
>So Mote It Be.

FOUR

The Chaste Moon

○ ◑ ● ◑ ○

The waking earth beneath the feet,
Lifeless winter must now retreat.
Time to fly in greatest haste,
When the Moon is round and when it's chaste.

The Full Moon in March is known as The Chaste Moon. This is the time to perform rituals dealing with chastity, the second chakra, new beginnings, happiness and good health, freedom, fertility, abundance, growth in every form, love and beauty, children in every aspect, the life force, good judgment, flowers and birds, psychic abilities, divination tools, dreams, mothers in general, and rituals that honor the Moon. It is a time to banish sickness, troubles in general, despair, and bad luck.

Flowers United

Coven Ritual (Pink)
by Aquila Eagle

MAGICKAL INTENTION: To beautify and send love into the world.

TIME: Full Moon in March, Venus Hour

TOOLS: One pink candle for each participant. Lovely oil, one two-foot length of twine for each participant, Venus incense, two flowers for each participant (use daisies, asters, hyacinths, or roses), and one piece of rose quartz for each person.

INSTRUCTIONS: Anoint the candles with Lovely oil, and use them to creat a circle around the cauldron that encompasses all of the participants and their tools. Have one participant tie all of the pieces of twine together into one big circle. Light the incense and the candles.

Have the person who tied the twine loop it over her left wrist, creating a figure eight with her wrist in the smaller loop of the eight. The participant on her left will then loop the twine around his left wrist in the same fashion. Continue around the circle until all the participants' left wrists are looped in the twine in a chain.

Each member should hold a flower in each hand and grasp a piece of the rose quartz with her or his right hand. Pass each flower in deosil motion through the incense smoke and recite the incantation as all participants hold hands. Raise all hands (still bound together and holding the flowers and rose quartzes) and visualize love and beauty streaming into each participant.

INCANTATION:

> All lives are intertwined,
> If only for a moment in time.
> We see each other every day,

Please show them all, love is the way.
Be beautiful within yourself,
So that all people can see that it cannot be helped.
This is the way the world should be,
To one another willingly.
Inside our souls for each other to know,
Lies unconditional love wherever we go.
To be great to even one child alone,
Is the ultimate gift worth passing on.
As we turn into beautiful flowers,
We are showing that our lives are not just ours.
Every scent and color around,
Joins us as one for we are bound.
As our roots unite and never part,
Just one moment in time is where it starts.
So Mote It Be.

○ ◐ ● ◑ ○

The Thought of Goddess

Solitary Ritual (Yellow)
by The Mighty Sheba

MAGICKAL INTENTION: To enhance mental abilities, to increase the memory, and to increase a positive attitude.

TIME: Full Moon in March, Venus hour

TOOLS: One large yellow candle, Goddess oil, Crystal Bell incense, a cold compress, and a comfortable place to lie down.

INSTRUCTIONS: Anoint the candle with Goddess oil. Light the candle and the incense. Rub the Goddess oil on your temples. Lie down, relax, and place the cold compress over your eyes. Meditate upon the Goddess. Ask Her to come into your mind. When you feel the presence of the Goddess, recite the incantation. Allow her to enter your mind. Either sleep will take you or you will have an incredible feeling of rejuvenation. Whichever way it hits you, the Goddess will bestow upon you a sense of health, well-being, and sharp mental abilities.

INCANTATION:

> The thought of Goddess,
> Enter my mind.
> Give to me,
> Your words so kind.
> Inspire my heart,
> Alert my brain.
> Enter me now,
> Your thoughts I gain.
> So Mote It Be.

○ ◑ ● ◐ ○

The Chastity Belt

Solitary or Coven Ritual (Blue)
by Sister Moon

MAGICKAL INTENTION: To promote chastity. This is an ancient ritual to be performed on this moon to ensure chastity for an upcoming marriage, which is usually in the month of June. The chastity belt is actually given to the groom from the bride as a gift on their wedding night. However, this ritual is not just to keep the female chaste; it works for the males, too. A groom in waiting should prepare the same belt for himself and give to his bride. This spell is also used to control sexual urges in general.

TIME: Full Moon in March, Saturn hour

TOOLS: One blue candle, Tranquillity oil, Purity incense, a narrow, black cord approximately seventy inches long (this will become the belt), two crystal beads, eighteen black beads, a white bead for each year of the intended wearer's age plus two extra, two ornate beads that represent the Goddess and the God, and one bead each in white, yellow, pink, blue, red, purple, green, orange, and silver.

INSTRUCTIONS: Anoint the candle with the oil. Light the candle and the incense. Tie a knot in one end of the cord. Add one crystal bead and tie a knot. Add the white, yellow, pink, blue, and red beads, tying a knot between each one. Add the God bead and tie a knot. Next, add nine of the black beads, knotting between each bead. Tie another knot, and add the white beads that represent the age of the person, with *no knots* in between the beads. Tie a knot, and add the nine remaining black beads, knotting between each bead. Tie another knot, add the Goddess bead and knot again. Add the purple, green, orange, silver, white, and the remaining crystal bead, knotting between each one. Knot the end to finish the belt.

Pass the belt through the incense smoke and recite the incantation. If you have been sexually active, wear the belt tied to the side. If you are a virgin, tie the belt in the front.

INCANTATION:
>When the full, round globe rises high in haste,
>Create the cinch for wedded-ones in chaste.
>If the wearer has tasted that of lust,

Then drape this belt to thy side in trust.
But if the blush of innocence is on thy face,
Then wear the girdled sash about the waist.
Bead the center for each year of thy life,
Add a crystal to the end to bless the wife.
After each bead is put into place,
Tie the knot to seal the fate.
An ivory token for purity of heart,
A topaz bead for good health and hearth.
A rose bead for love to guide the course,
A sapphire bead to protect the source.
A ruby-red bead to summon desire,
A token to God and all he inspires.
Then place a string of ebony,
To mark the future and destiny.
A token to Goddess and Her powers that beam,
Then nine ebony more for thy children's dreams.
A violet bead for the enchanted elf,
A jade bead for the common wealth.
A salmon bead for marriage attraction,
And worn Handfasting day as fashion.
A silver token for chastity's sake,
An ivory bead for heaven's gate.
A crystal orb for magickal treasures,
Adorn your life from now till forever.
If a knot is missed when sash has end,
Then one wish placed will then be banned.
Nimble fingers will weave thy fate,
And determine the future of wedded mate.
The same for husband who is wed to the Witch,
When spun of chaste on thread of pitch.
So Mote It Be.

○ ◑ ● ◐ ○

Soul Release

Solitary or Coven Ritual (White)
by Nova

MAGICKAL INTENTION: To release and forget things that are troubling you.

TIME: Full Moon in March, Saturn hour

TOOLS: One yellow candle, Forgiveness oil, Eucalyptus incense, and several pieces of white paper.

INSTRUCTIONS: Anoint the candle with the oil. Light the candle and the incense. On separate pieces of paper, write down the things that are troubling you. Shred them and release them into the wind while reciting the incantation. (If no wind exists, a fan will do the trick.) Repeat as many times as there are pieces of paper. Soon, all your troubles will be gone.

INCANTATION:
>As these troubles break and fly
>>away,
>
>Release the soul from its stay.
>In a prison of painful feelings,
>Let the soul begin the healing.
>So Mote It Be.

○ ◑ ● ◐ ○

Seven Powers

Solitary or Coven (Purple)
by Leebrah

MAGICKAL INTENTION: To open the third eye.

TIME: The Hare Moon in March, Moon hour

TOOLS: One large purple candle, Seven Powers oil, Moon incense, two pinches each of cabbage, pepperwort (or peppercorn), gourd, jasmine, and mushroom, a mortar and pestle, and one red flannel mojo.

INSTRUCTIONS: Anoint the candle with the oil. Light the candle and the incense. Combine all the herbs and grind them together with a mortar and pestle. Place them into the mojo and tie it shut. Pass the mojo in deosil motion three times through the incense smoke and recite the incantation. Place the mojo beneath your pillow and allow the energies to flow to your third eye while you sleep.

INCANTATION:

> Window be open to my soul,
> Increase seven powers is my goal.
> With the tarot, a pendulum, the runes or ball,
> Whatever the choice, the desire is to know all.
> Purity is a bountiful part,
> Hope is for the love in all hearts.
> Protection from wrong is what I seek,
> Wisdom of knowing the difference is not meek.
> Enlightenment be on display,
> While visions in front of me show the way.
> With psychic abilities coming into view,

The understanding will, too.
With all the odds in my favor,
The course of luck and prosperity will endeavor.
The Hag's Hare Moon abound tonight,
So the Goddess can show me the light.
So Mote It Be.

○ ◐ ● ◑ ○

Just for Laughs

Coven Ritual (Yellow)
by Queen of the Meadow

MAGICKAL INTENTION: To promote happiness and good health for children. (For children between the ages of six and thirteen)

TIME: Full Moon in March, Sun hour

TOOLS: One yellow candle, Positive Attitude oil, Joy incense, a comedy script, and a tape recorder.

INSTRUCTIONS: Anoint the candle with the oil. Light the candle and the incense. The comedy script should be prepared ahead of time. Create the script to be for as many children as you want to include in this. One of my favorite scripts was "Who's on First" as performed by Abbot and Costello. You can always write your own script.

Tape-record everything in the script, without trying to make it perfect. Allow the screw-ups and instant laughter. Then (without the children present) recite the incantation over the tape and put it away for another time.

Don't replay the recording until one of the children is sick, lonely, or troubled. Hearing his own laughter will instantly make the child laugh and cure whatever ails him.

INCANTATION:
> Capture the laughter and hold it there,
> Children cured of blues and despair.
> Share good health and heal the child,
> Bless the days of running wild.
> So Mote It Be.

○ ◐ ● ◑ ○

Hag's Hair

Solitary Ritual (Pink)
by Sister Moon

MAGICKAL INTENTION: To make your hair more beautiful.

TIME: Hag's Hare Moon, just before Venus hour

TOOLS: A hairbrush, one pink candle, Goddess oil, Venus incense, a mortar and pestle, a dash of lemon juice, three tablespoons of flaxseed oil, one brown egg, three tablespoons of maidenhair, a pinch of ground ginseng, plastic wrap, shampoo, conditioner, and three gallons of rainwater.

INSTRUCTIONS: Bend over at the waist and brush your hair upside down for one hundred strokes, making sure the scalp is stimulated and all residues of styling aids are gone. Anoint the candle with the oil. Light the candle and the incense.

Place the lemon juice, flaxseed oil, egg, maidenhair, and ginseng in the mortar, and grind with the pestle until the potion is gooey. When the Venus hour approaches, recite the incantation over the potion.

Work the potion into your hair until it is completely saturated. Place the plastic wrap over your hair and let it sit. Go outside and soak up the sun. Feel the potion tingling and revitalizing your hair.

After one hour, shampoo and condition your hair with your normal hair products. When you are ready to do your final rinse of the conditioner from your hair, thoroughly rinse your head in the rainwater. Allow your hair to air-dry naturally. You will see an incredible improvement in your hair instantly.

INCANTATION:

> Potion of Witches with beautiful hair,
> Adorn my head beyond compare.
> Rich and thick the potion goes,
> Absorb the sunshine and the glow.
> Maidens weave the gorgeous threads,
> That creates the hair upon my head.
> Combine the egg, magick, and grain,
> And rinse me beautiful with Isis rain.
> So Mote It Be.

FIVE

Ostara

Ostara's melody on the wings of Spirit,
The Witch's heart extends to hear it.
The drumming nature of the life force,
Riding with passion upon the white horse.

Ostara is on March 21 or March 22 and is a minor Sabbat. This is the time to perform rituals dealing with life, health and healing, reconciling differences, dedication and purpose, growth in all areas, new beginnings, adventures, excitement, positive energy, wisdom and intelligence, chance on any level, inspiration, fertility, balance, maturity, planting and seeding, animals, and happiness.

The Ostara Chandelier

Solitary or Coven ritual (Rainbow Magick)
by Aquila Eagle

MAGICKAL INTENTION: To experience growth on all levels of existence.

TIME: March 21 or 22, Mars hour

TOOLS: One multicolored candle, Honeysuckle oil, Dragon's Blood incense, five sturdy, large, naturally fallen branches of a similar size (thistle works great), twine, five pieces of parchment in blue, purple, green, gold, and pink, potting soil, five small pots, and eight seeds each of snapdragon, basil, tarragon, ginger, and bloodroot.

INSTRUCTIONS: Anoint the candle with the oil. Light the candle and the incense. Create a pentagram with the branches and tie them together tightly with the twine at each of the corners.

On the blue parchment, write: "All will arise and enter to find, snapdragons with protection in mind." Fill one pot halfway with soil, and add the snapdragon seeds. Anoint the blue parchment with Honeysuckle oil.

On the green parchment, write: "A prosperous future is in the leaves, that basil provides willingly." Fill a second pot halfway with soil and add the basil seeds. Anoint the green parchment with Honeysuckle oil.

On the purple parchment, write: "Psychic powers will grow in time, with help from the scent of tarragon." Fill a third pot halfway with soil and add the tarragon seeds. Anoint the purple parchment with Honeysuckle oil.

On the gold parchment, write: "With ginger roots fixed and strong, there will be success to follow along." Fill the fourth pot halfway with soil and add the ginger seeds. Anoint the gold parchment with Honeysuckle oil.

On the pink parchment, write: "Showers of love for those who wait, for perfect bloodroot to awake." Fill the fifth pot halfway with soil and add the bloodroot seeds. Anoint the pink parchment with Honeysuckle oil.

Pass all five parchments through the incense smoke and recite the incantation. Set each parchment alight with the flame of the multicolored candle, and allow them to burn to ash, keeping the ashes separate.

After the ashes have cooled, place them with the seeds of the appropriate pot (ashes of the blue parchment go in the pot with the snapdragon seeds, for example). Fill the pots the rest of the way with soil and water them. Place each pot in one of the slots made by the five points of the branch pentagram and hang it as a decorative chandelier near a window with southern exposure. As the seeds grow, so will all of the areas of your life.

INCANTATION:

>Equal in time, between day and night, new life
>>begins under both lights.
>All will arise and enter to find, snapdragons with
>>protection in mind.
>A prosperous future is in the leaves, that basil
>>provides willingly.
>Psychic powers will grow in time, with help
>>from the scent of tarragon.
>With ginger roots fixed and strong, there will be
>>success to follow along.

Showers of love for those who wait, for perfect
   bloodroot to awake.
Thistle for strength to hold us strong, while
   Dragon's Blood has good intentions.
Soft with a touch of gentleness, honeysuckle is
   the kiss.
New life begins all around, while in the shape of
   the crown.
So Mote It Be.

○ ◑ ● ◐ ○

The Tree of Life

Coven Ritual (Green)
by Sister Moon

MAGICKAL INTENTION: To bring positive energy.

TIME: March 21 or 22, Sun hour

TOOLS: One green candle, White Solstice oil and incense, two brooms, three pieces of white parchment for each participant, and a fruit bearing tree.

INSTRUCTIONS: Anoint the candle with the oil. Light the candle and the incense. Cast a full circle with a full Call of Order.

Open the front door and the back door of the Covenstead; the High Priestess should stand at the front door, and the youngest or newest member should stand at the back door. Using one of the brooms, the High Priestess should sweep into the Covenstead the new and positive energy, while at the back door the youngest member uses the other broom to sweep out the negative energy. While this is happening, all participants should recite Incantation One three times. Close the doors.

Next, each participant should write on the parchment three things he or she would like to see grow in his or her life. Take the candle and the wishes outside and gather in a circle around the fruit tree. Set the wishes alight with candle flame, and allow each one to burn to ash. Scatter the ashes near the roots of the tree. All participants should now hold hands and circle the tree once in de-osil motion while reciting Incantation Two.

INCANTATION ONE:

> Positive sweep the energy in,
> A bright new year now begins.
> Negative sweep the energy out,
> Never return or creep about.
> So Mote It Be.

INCANTATION TWO:

> Tree of Life, wishes of three,
> Grow and blossom from this tree.
> Young and new the energy grows,
> Blessed by Goddess above and below.
> Ashes be scattered by base and root,
> Trunk be strong by head and foot.
> Garden of Life, bless this tree,
> Accept this offering of our wishes three.
> So Mote It Be.

○ ◔ ● ◑ ○

Astra's Energy

Solitary or Coven Ritual (Purple)
by Astra

MAGICKAL INTENTION: To bring empowering energy to your physical and emotional being.

TIME: March 21 or 22, Moon hour

TOOLS: One purple candle, Black Cat oil, Joy incense, two pinches each of angelica, cinnamon, Echinacea, ginger, hawthorne, and basil, a mortar and pestle, and a small decorative box.

INSTRUCTIONS: Anoint the candle with the Black Cat oil. Light the candle and the incense. Grind the herbs using the mortar and pestle. Keeping the herbs in the mortar, pass them three times in deosil motion through the incense smoke. Place the herbs in the decorative box, and pass it in deosil motion through the incense smoke while reciting the incantation three times. Seal the box with the Black Cat oil. Whenever you need a boost, open the box and inhale the potion.

INCANTATION:

> As the moon shines its wondrous beauty,
> The power of three times three calls a duty.
> The flames reach high with intensity,
> As the negative energy loses its density.
> Let happiness and rebirth join my heart,
> May this joyful feeling never part.
> With each tiresome feeling,
> Open the energized box and feel the
> healing.

The moon shines bright with beauty,
And now, so do I.
So Mote It Be.

○ ◐ ● ◑ ○

Wisdom's Fire

Coven Ritual (Orange/Gold)
by Lyra

MAGICKAL INTENTION: To bring about wisdom and to access a higher intelligence.

TIME: March 21 or 22, Mercury hour

TOOLS: One white candle for each participant, Honeysuckle oil, a small bonfire, Draw Across incense, a unity candle, and a large bowl filled with lavender, broomtops, and savory herbs.

INSTRUCTIONS: Anoint the candles with the oil. Cast a full circle around the bonfire. The High Priestess lights the incense and passes one white candle to each participant.

The High Priestess lights her white candle from the unity candle, and then uses her candle to light that of each participant. She will then take a handful of the herbs and scatter them into the bonfire and will recite the incantation. The High Priestess then passes the bowl of herbs to each member and they all follow the same procedure. All participants link hands and breathe in the contemplation and thankfulness for the gift of wisdom that they are receiving.

INCANTATION:

> The golden wisdom of three times law,
> Be here with us now within this call.
> Open our minds to possess,
> The wisdom of Solomon and Moses.
> I toss these herbs into the fire,
> Increase our wisdom and lift us higher.
> Give us grace and purity of heart,
> Be with us always and never part.
> So Mote It Be.

○ ◐ ● ◐ ○

Connection

Solitary or Coven Ritual (Pink)
by Nova

MAGICKAL INTENTION: To reconcile differences with an old friend.

TIME: March 21 or 22, Mercury hour

TOOLS: One pink candle, Friendship oil, Purity incense, a turquoise stone, a piece of pink paper with your friend's name written on it, and one red mojo.

INSTRUCTIONS: Anoint the candle with Friendship oil. Light the candle and incense. Visualize you and your friend talking things out and forgiving each other. Place the turquoise stone and paper in the mojo. Pass the mojo in deosil motion three times through the incense smoke while reciting the incantation.

Carry the mojo with you until the friendship has rekindled. Then bury the mojo beneath a weeping willow tree and recite the incantation one final time.

INCANTATION:

A turquoise stone to find
Harmony and peace, leave behind
Differences, disagreements, and hurt.
The connection of true friendship will not part.
Let pink burn bright,
To reconcile this fight.
So Mote It Be.

○ ◐ ● ◑ ○

The Million-Dollar Wealth Spell

Solitary or Coven Ritual (Green)
by Shanatawah

MAGICKAL INTENTION: To bring great wealth and abundance.

TIME: March 21 or 22, Jupiter hour

TOOLS: One green candle, Emerald oil, Prosperity incense, a picture of a hundred dollar bill on green paper, a piece of malachite, a pinch of comfrey, and one red mojo.

INSTRUCTIONS: Anoint the candle with Emerald oil. Light the candle and the incense. Wrap the picture around the malachite and pass it in deosil motion through the incense smoke; recite the incantation. Place the paper-wrapped malachite in the red mojo and add the pinch of comfrey. Place the mojo in a garden.

INCANTATION:

> Around the stone of malachite,
> Wraps one hundred very tight.
> So one million times the wealth will come,
> With this spell, it is done.
> So Mote It Be.

○ ◑ ● ◐ ○

I'm So Excited!

Solitary or Coven Ritual (Red)
by Crystal Ball

MAGICKAL INTENTION: To feel excitement, enthusiasm, and all-around terrific. This spell works great on people who are too serious. The prism holds an incredible spectrum of magick, enthusiasm, and excitement. This spell helps you extract its energy.

TIME: March 21 or 22, Mars hour

TOOLS: One red candle, Fire of Passion oil, Black Cat incense, a prism two to four inches long, a piece of clear thread or fishing line from which to suspend the prism, and a dark cloth.

INSTRUCTIONS: Anoint the candle with Fire of Passion oil. Light the candle and the incense. Pass the prism four times in deosil motion through the incense smoke. Recite the incantation.

Hang the prism from the thread or fishing line in a room that has a southern exposure. Leave it there for four days, each day reciting the incantation. On the fifth day, wrap the prism in a dark cloth and place it where it will not be disturbed.

When you are ready to use it, recite the incantation again, and hang it in any room you desire. (Be forewarned, if you put it in your bedroom, you may not be able to sleep well there!)

INCANTATION:

> Unleash the power of Black Cat,
> For exciting energy to attract.
> Dimensions facing a southern Sun,
> Absorbs the magick of having fun.
> Four days south and then in dark,
> Incubates the magick of a child's heart.
> Hang the orb within the room,
> Excitement release Ostara's Moon.
> So Mote It Be.

SIX

The Seed Moon

○ ◐ ● ◑ ○

Gargoyles and dragons will till the soil,
Preparing the earth for the toil.
To bear the fruit from seed to feast,
And all the magick that rise due east.

The Full Moon in April is known as The Seed Moon. This is a time to perform rituals dealing with planting, seeds of all kinds, the third chakra, weather magick, gargoyles, dragons, unicorns and other mythical beasts, beauty, truth, originality, balance, travel adventures, protection during travel, progress, any type of entrepreneurship, advancements, goals, investments, and positive decisions. It is also a time to banish anger, sadness, darkness, and any issues that involve hate.

Fly by Night

Solitary or Coven Ritual (Blue)
by Ivy

MAGICKAL INTENTION: For protection when traveling by air.

TIME: Seed Moon in April, Moon hour

TOOLS: One blue candle, Protection oil, Dove's Flight incense, three pieces of star anise, three pinches of hyssop, a piece of pyrite, and one red flannel mojo.

INSTRUCTIONS: Anoint the candle with Protection oil. Light the candle and the incense. Place the star anise, the hyssop, and the pyrite in the mojo. Add three drops of the Protection oil and three pinches of unlit incense to the mojo. Pull the strings closed and knot the bag three times. Pass the mojo in deosil motion through the incense smoke, and recite the incantation three times. Keep the mojo in your pocket when flying.

INCANTATION:

> Three pinches each of herbs
> for flight,
> With pyrite in a mojo tight.
> With protection and a pinch
> of flight,
> Arrive safely and everything
> is all right.
> So Mote It Be.

○ ◐ ● ◑ ○

Devil's Eggs

Coven Ritual (Yellow)
by Sister Moon

MAGICKAL INTENTION: To banish sadness and darkness from your life; to promote rapid changes and destroy stagnation and indecision.

TIME: Seed Moon in April, Mercury hour

TOOLS: Thirteen yellow candles, Springtime oil, Positive Attitude incense, a sharp yellow crayon for each participant, thirteen hard-boiled eggs, two teaspoons of red food coloring, two tablespoons vinegar, a black bowl, a yellow bowl, four tablespoons of mayonnaise, three teaspoons of prepared mustard, a pinch of salt, a pinch of pepper, and a big splash of dill pickle juice.

INSTRUCTIONS: Anoint the candles with the Springtime oil. Light the candles and the incense. Using yellow crayons, each participant should write on an egg what has kept him or her in sadness, anger, darkness, or in stalemate.

Place the red food coloring and the vinegar in the black bowl and add the thirteen eggs. In the yellow bowl, mix the mayonnaise, mustard, salt, pepper, and pickle juice, and set aside.

After all of the hard-boiled eggs in the black bowl have turned red from the dye, each participant should reclaim his or her egg. See how visible the written problems are. All participants now hold hands and recite the incantation. Each person should pick up his or her egg and start chipping away at the shell while visualizing the problem breaking away as the shell does. Cut each egg in half, remove the yolks, and place them in the yellow bowl with the mayonnaise mixture. Combine them well, and fill all the egg whites with the yolks. Give each participant two halves.

Hold hands again and recite the incantation one final time. As you eat the eggs, visualize your problems turning inside out until they are no longer visible.

INCANTATION:

As thirteen is a positive flow,
Anger and troubles now must go.
Upon the egg in a yellow hue,
I write the words that I cut in two.
No longer red in stagnation torn,
For my life is whole and now reborn.
I cleanse with springtime for purity,
I add positive attitude for certainty.
The juice of green for my growth,
Combined together with the yoke.
Out you go! Demons be gone!
Take these problems and your pawn.
I peel away your wicked spell,
And cast you back to darkened hell.
Eggs of Devil are now set free,
I cast this spell for serenity.
Eggs of yellow and of white,
Absorb the powers of the light!
Balance will flow as I ingest,
Progress and joy are my quest.
Life with bounty set in motion,
I accept the fate of this potion.
Visions and path is all I see,
This is my will, So Mote It Be.

○ ◐ ● ◐ ○

Stormy

Coven Ritual (Purple)
by Phoenix

MAGICKAL INTENTION: To conjure rain. This spell is to aid the earth in times of drought.

TIME: Full Moon in April, Moon hour

TOOLS: One purple candle for each participant, High John the Conqueror oil, Mandrake incense, a large cauldron full of water, and a Witch's broom for each participant.

INSTRUCTIONS: Anoint the candles with the oil. Light the candles and the incense. Cast a circle and place the candles around the cauldron.

Each Witch should dip his or her broom into the cauldron, saturating it with water. Divide the circle into four quadrants—East, South, West, and North. The participants standing in the East of the circle should shake their brooms into the air while reciting the Incantation of the East. Proceed in deosil motion through the directions, with the participants in each quadrant shaking their brooms and reciting the appropriate incantation.

When everyone is finished, all participants should cross broom over broom and shout, "So Mote It Be."

INCANTATION OF THE EAST:

> Watchtowers of the East,
> Goddess, please shed tears of rain.
> Storm the earth with moisture,
> We ask in her name,
> Diana!

INCANTATION OF THE SOUTH:

> Watchtowers of the South,
> Goddess, please shed tears of rain.
> Storm the earth with moisture,
> We ask in her name,
> Diana!

INCANTATION OF THE WEST:

> Watchtowers of the West,
> Goddess, please shed tears of rain.
> Storm the earth with moisture,
> We ask in her name,
> Diana!

INCANTATION OF THE NORTH:

> Watchtowers of the North,
> Goddess, please shed tears of rain.
> Storm the earth with moisture,
> We ask in her name,
> Diana!

○ ◐ ● ◑ ○

Anger, Be Gone

Solitary or Coven Ritual (Gray/Blue)
by Ariel

MAGICKAL INTENTION: To dispel anger and hate.

TIME: Full Moon in April, Moon hour

TOOLS: One gray candle, one blue candle, Rose Cross oil, Tranquillity incense, one pinch each of bay leaf, fennel, horseradish, hyssop, onion, and yucca, and one red flannel mojo.

INSTRUCTIONS: Anoint both candles with Rose Cross oil. Light the candles and the incense. Place all of the herbs into the mojo and pass it widdershins (counterclockwise) ten times through the incense smoke while reciting the incantation. Tie the mojo closed and bury it where you will never see it again.

INCANTATION:

> Thoughts of darkness must now take flight,
> The anger and hate will purge with white.
> In our lives we need not,
> Bitter images of our thoughts.
> From our minds and our hearts,
> Send to light what was dark.
> Lift our souls in love and light,
> Clear our spirits and make them bright.
> So Mote It Be.

Beautiful

Solitary Ritual (Pink)
by The Mighty Sheba

MAGICKAL INTENTION: To become more beautiful.

TIME: Full Moon in April, Venus hour

TOOLS: One pink candle, Lovely oil, Lovely incense, one cup of uncooked oatmeal, one tablespoon of lemon juice, one egg white, an earthen bowl, spring water, and a man's shaving brush.

INSTRUCTIONS: Anoint the candle with Lovely oil. Light the candle and the incense. Place the oatmeal, lemon juice, and egg white in the bowl and mix well. Add the spring water sparingly and until mixture is the consistency of a thick paste. Recite the incantation over the mixture, and apply to your face with the shaving brush. Allow it to dry. Wash it off with additional spring water. Your face will have a healthy, beautiful glow.

INCANTATION:

> Lovely is the face I see,
> Lovely glows outwardly.
> Within this bowl I create the paste,
> That puts the beauty on my face.
> So Mote It Be.

Gargoyles at the Gate

Solitary Ritual (Blue)
by Sister Moon

MAGICKAL INTENTION: To protect your home or business from negative people.

TIME: Full Moon in April, Saturn hour

TOOLS: Four blue candles, Protection oil, Protection incense, and four ceramic gargoyles.

INSTRUCTIONS: Anoint the candles with the Protection oil. Place the four gargoyles in each of the four directions. Place a candle beside each gargoyle. Wave incense smoke over each gargoyle and recite the incantation. Whenever you feel danger is near, light the candles so the gargoyles will watch over your area.

INCANTATION:
>Positioned at the towers and gates,
>Gargoyles watch in earnest haste.
>For the protection of the house and grounds,
>And all the things of sight and sound.
>Keep us safe from danger and harm,
>Watch over us in every storm.
>Jump from the rooftops if in need,
>To frighten away all evil deeds.
>So Mote It Be.

Decisions of Taste and Flavor

Solitary Ritual (Green/Yellow)
by Journey

MAGICKAL INTENTION: To help you make a positive decision.

TIME: Full Moon in April, Mercury hour

TOOLS: Two green candles, High Meadows oil, a four-inch square piece of green paper, Huntress incense, a pinch each of dried parsley, dried oregano, dried marjoram, dried mint, and dried mace, a small aventurine, a red flannel mojo, and a piece of white string twenty-inches long.

INSTRUCTIONS: Anoint the green candles with the High Meadows oil and place them in the center of the paper. Light the candles and the incense. Sprinkle the herbs around the candles while concentrating on the decision you need to make. Remove the candles from the paper. Fold the herbs into the paper in a small bundle and place the paper and aventurine into the mojo. Pass the mojo in deosil motion through the incense smoke. Repeat the incantation four times.

Tie the string around the mojo and make it into a necklace. Anoint the mojo with the oil and seal it with a kiss. Wear it over your heart until you are clear about the right decision. When you are, bury the mojo on the next hare moon.

INCANTATION:

> Positive decisions of taste and flavor,
> Positive decision to gain God's favor.
> A mix of it all this magickal hour,
> For my decision to grow and flower.
> Parsley for purification.
> Oregano for love, marjoram for healing.
> Mint and mace for psychic power.
> Aventurine to increase perception.
> Lend this decision its depth and feeling.
> Sealed with a kiss,
> And worn by my heart.
> Make this decision positive,
> From the start.
> So Mote It Be.

SEVEN

Beltane

Abandon weaved baskets by the front door,
Flirting and seducing the one you adore.
Bareback horses and afternoon rides,
Conjures a spell that makes you a bride.

Beltane is on May 1 and is a major Sabbat. This is a time to perform rituals dealing with beauty, wealth, fertility, sexuality, passion, house and home, receiving help of any kind to make differences in your life, growth of any kind, help in obtaining difficult things, faery magick, cleansing, ancient mystics, spirit guides, purification, tools, laurels and textiles, web magick, potions, merriment and entertainment, physical energy, endurance, and courage.

The Ancient Ones

Solitary or Coven Ritual (Blue)
by Tatituba

MAGICKAL INTENTION: To ask and receive help on any level.

TIME: May 1, Mercury hour

TOOLS: One blue candle, one yellow candle, Helping Hand oil, Helping Hand incense, a Helping Hand root, a pinch of mandrake, a pen with blue ink, a picture of what you need help with, and a red flannel mojo.

INSTRUCTIONS: Anoint both candles with the Helping Hand oil. Light the candles and the incense. Write in blue ink on the back of the picture exactly what it is you need help with. Place the picture, the Helping Hand root, and the mandrake inside the red flannel mojo. Anoint the bag with the Helping Hand oil and recite the incantation. Take the mojo to the gates of a graveyard and bury it there. Recite the incantation over the mojo once again. Leave the area and know that help is on its way.

INCANTATION:

> Ancient Ones—
> I ask for your help.
> I offer this mojo,
> In your name.
> Oh Ancient Ones—
> I need your assistance.
> Peer into this earth,
> And open your heart

To aid me.
So Mote It Be.

○ ◐ ● ◐ ○

The Beltane Basket

Coven Ritual (Green)
by Sister Moon

MAGICKAL INTENTION: For bounty and prosperity.

TIME: May 1, Jupiter hour

TOOLS: One white candle, one red candle, Temple of Light oil, Huntress incense, one large, brightly colored basket, fresh flowers for the altar, a small basket for each participant, sunflower seeds, a red-and-white checkered tablecloth and napkins, and red and white plates. Each participant should bring food to be shared, like hardboiled or deviled eggs, bread and cheese, red and white wine, fresh fruits, and so on. Recruit a Coven member (or invite a guest) with musical talent to play his or her instrument at the ritual.

INSTRUCTIONS: This ritual is a festive feast, and needs to be held outdoors in sacred space that has some sort of table, or enough room to place the food on a cloth on the ground. The table setting should include the tablecloth, napkins, and red and white plates. Anoint the candles with the oil and place them in the center of the table. Set out the food. Light the candles and the incense, but keep the incense about twelve feet to the east of the table.

After the table is set, each participant should prepare a plate of food and set it in front of her or him. Instruct the musician to begin playing; each member circles the table as in "musical chairs." When the music stops, each participant sits down wherever he or she happens to be. Recite the incantation, wish each other a blessed journey into prosperity, and enjoy the food.

When everyone is finished, set the table with the large, Beltane basket at one place on the table and repeat the game of "musical chairs." Whoever sits at the place where the basket is will receive the largest bounty for the year. This person will be responsible for bringing three items to the next feast: the red wine, the white wine, and enough bread for everyone. The Beltane basket is never to be empty as long as it is in someone's possession.

Place the sunflower seeds and pieces of leftover fruit, bread, and so on in the smallest baskets. When the feast is over, walk unusual paths to share the bounty in the small baskets with the animals and to mark the trail with the sunflower seeds to signify the "path to bounty."

INCANTATION:

> Beltane Basket in all your splendor,
> Bounty and beauty from the
>   Sender.
> Feast in gardens among flowers
>   and trees,
> Ensuring happiness and prosperity.
> So Mote It Be.

○ ◐ ● ◑ ○

Web of Dreams

Solitary Ritual (Orange)
by Indigo

MAGICKAL INTENTION: To obtain something that you need.

TIME: May 1, Sun hour

TOOLS: An undisturbed outdoor spider's web, one orange candle, Scorpion oil, Tiger incense, a cup of salt, and a small chicken feather.

INSTRUCTIONS: Go to the spider's web. Anoint the candle with Scorpion oil. Light the candle and the incense. Make a circle of salt around the area of the web. Place the orange candle inside the circle. While holding the feather in your power hand, visualize exactly what it is you want. Imagine your need going into the feather. Recite the incantation. Release the feather from your hand so it gets caught in the web. Your wish will be caught as long as the spider is not disturbed by having it there.

INCANTATION:

> Little spider with web so strong,
> Captures all that comes along.
> With your help, I shall receive,
> All the things that I so need.
> Feather and salt to help you snare,
> Things for me if you dare.
> Bring to me this Beltane day,
> All I ask and all I pray.
> So Mote It Be.

○ ◑ ● ◐ ○

Great Balls of Fire

Coven Ritual (Red)
by Rising Star

MAGICKAL INTENTION: For absolute courage.

TIME: May 1, Mars hour

TOOLS: One red candle for each participant, Mandrake oil, Witch incense, three crystal balls, and a dark cloth.

INSTRUCTIONS: Anoint the candles with the Mandrake oil. Light the candles and the incense. Three participants should each pick up a crystal ball and pass it through the incense smoke; then each should extend their crystal ball to the south. Recite the incantation four times, ending with "So Mote It Be."

Keep the balls wrapped in a dark cloth until they are needed. When someone is in need of great courage, that person should take the crystal balls to their home and drain their energy. When done, the crystal balls should be reenergized the next Beltane.

INCANTATION:

> I charge thee, Crystals, with the power,
> With courage and strength from the
> Southern Tower.

○ ◑ ● ◐ ○

The Letter I Seals the Trust

Solitary Ritual (Red)
by Poseidon

MAGICKAL INTENTION: Helps to conquer the fear of intimacy.

TIME: May 1, Venus hour

TOOLS: A sharp knife, two red taper candles, Sweetheart oil, Fire of Passion incense, a piece of pink parchment, a pen with black ink, a pink envelope, and two wax-seal stamps, one with your first initial and one with that of your partner.

INSTRUCTIONS: With the sharp knife, carve your name in one of the red candles. Carve your partner's name in the other. Anoint the candles with Sweetheart oil. Light the candles and the incense.

Using the pen and parchment, write a letter to your partner expressing your desire to know him or her intimately. Write about sharing your dreams, goals, and plans. Express your willingness to commit to your relationship even when times are tough. Express your love for your partner.

When you are finished, place the parchment into the envelope and seal it. Using the wax of the two red candles, drip the wax on the back of the envelope and use the seal with your initial, and then that of your partner to assure closure of the envelope. Pass the envelope through the incense smoke and recite the incantation.

Give the envelope to your partner. When he or she breaks open the wax seal, the spell will begin.

INCANTATION:

> Ignite the Fire of Passion,
> Not for money or fashion.

Write on parchment pink,
The words of midnight ink.
Thoughts of intimate desire,
Sparks the lover's fire.
Hopes and wishes so dear,
Removes all of her/[his] fears.
Carefully bound and sealed,
With initials that you wield.
Give to lover and seal is broken
This spell is now forever opened.
So Mote It Be.

○ ◐ ● ◑ ○

GROW, GROW, GROW!

Coven Ritual (Purple)
by Willow

MAGICKAL INTENTION: A Beltane potion for positive growth.

TIME: May 1, Jupiter hour

TOOLS: One yellow candle, one red candle, one white candle, White Solstice oil and incense, one pinch each of lavender, chamomile, meadowsweet, and spearmint, a mortar and pestle, a quart of water, a tea steeper, and a bathtub.

INSTRUCTIONS: Anoint all of the candles with White Solstice oil. Light the candles and the incense. Place all of the herbs in the mortar and grind them well. Visualize the positive growth you would like to see in yourself. See your positive qualities becoming even greater. Visualize all the negative things flowing away from you. Heat the water and bring to a boil. Take half of the herbs, place them in the tea steeper and brew. Take the other half of the herbs and place them in the bathtub full of warm water along with three drops of White Solstice oil. Bring your tea into the bathroom and enjoy your bath. As you are drinking the tea, recite the incantation and allow this spell to work its magick both inside and out.

INCANTATION:

As the beginning of the warm season arrives,
Rebirth and change are not denied.
The May Queen and Her King assist,
My journey to eternal bliss.
This potion I drink will mark the start,
Of rebirth and celebration in my heart.
The Almighty Goddess and God will show,
Within me, possibility, happiness and peace will grow.
This is my will, So Mote It Be.

○ ◐ ● ◑ ○

Let the Games Begin!

Solitary or Coven Ritual (Yellow)
by Sister Moon

MAGICKAL INTENTION: A spell to make a party wonderful and fun.

TIME: May 1, Sun hour

TOOLS: One yellow candle, Joy incense, Merry Meet oil, three cups of paper confetti, a handwritten agenda of the party, a cauldron, and a small decorative box.

INSTRUCTIONS: Anoint the candle with Merry Meet oil. Light the candle and the incense. Pass the confetti and the agenda through the incense smoke. Anoint the agenda with the oil, set it alight using the candle flame, and allow it to burn out in the cauldron. While the agenda is burning, pass the confetti through the agenda smoke. Recite the incantation. Go outside and throw half of the confetti into the wind. Place the rest of the confetti in the small box and put the box in the room that the party will be in. (If the party is on a different day than May 1, keep the box in the dark until the day of the party.) Your party will be fun and fabulous.

INCANTATION:

> A time of frolic,
> A time to play.
> Bless the night,
> And the day.
> Festive party,
> Beltane blessed.
> All be merry,
> Each friend and guest.
> So Mote It Be.

EIGHT

The Lovers' Moon

The maidens churn a lover's brew,
Potions and notions for love that is true.
Anxious and waiting for a charming knight,
That she conjured on lover's night.

The Full Moon in May is known as The Lovers' Moon. This is a time to perform rituals dealing with love, lovers, female energies, sex, home, family, old and new relationships, friendships, renewed energy of mind, body, and spirit, the physical body, cleansing in general, employment, prosperity, wealth in all forms, abundance, hopefulness, good judgment, laurels and crowns, and rituals that honor the Witch as Maiden, Mother, and Crone. This is also the time to banish solemnity, loneliness, and debts of any kind.

Calm Waters

Solitary Ritual (Pink)
by Lyra

MAGICKAL INTENTION: Ritual cleansing to relax and inspire the mind, body, and spirit.

TIME: Lovers' Moon, Jupiter Hour

TOOLS: A bathtub, three tablespoons of Lemon Drops bath salts, a pinch each of apple, cardamom, daisy, geranium, orchid, peach, plum, rose, and spearmint, one white candle, one yellow candle, one blue candle, one purple candle, Blessed Be oil, and Meditation incense.

INSTRUCTIONS: Fill the bathtub with extra warm water, sprinkle in the bath salts, and the herbs. Anoint the candles with the oil. Place the white candle in the east, the yellow in the south, the blue in the west, and the purple in the north. Light the candles and incense, and ease your body into the bathwater. Recite the incantation.

This relaxing ritual will allow you to unwind, release the negative energies of the day, and allow you to love yourself once again.

INCANTATION:

> To the Goddess, be with me now.
> Surround me with love.
> Lift my mind and spirit,
> To unlimited heights above.
> Give my body health and strength,
> Keep me pure to do Thy bidding.
> Let me shine with true light and love,

Give me wings to fly as the dove.
So Mote It Be.

○ ◐ ● ◑ ○

Lady and Lord Laurels

Coven Ritual (Pink)
by Sister Moon

MAGICKAL INTENTION: To become more beautiful by adorning yourself with a laurel crown.

TIME: Full Moon in May, Venus hour

TOOLS: Three pink candles, Venus oil, Goddess incense, three different kinds or colors of flowers (fresh, silk or dried), sprigs of baby's breath, feathers, pearl beads, a wire wreath base to wrap the flowers around, and ribbons in three different colors.

INSTRUCTIONS: Anoint the candles with Venus oil. Light the candles and the incense. Cast a full circle and sit comfortably within it; lay all of your supplies in the middle of the circle to share with the other participants.

Start creating your laurel by wrapping the flowers around the circular wire that will crown your head. Visualize yourself walking in the beautiful Garden of the Goddess. See yourself taking the time to smell the beautiful flowers that the spring has given you. Visualize yourself looking exactly as you desire. Finish your laurel of flowers by adding the ribbons so they stream down the back. Make sure you help any other members that seem to be having trouble. Pass your laurel through the incense smoke as you recite the incantation. As you place the laurel upon your head, you will instantly become as beautiful as you visualized.

INCANTATION:

> Lady so lovely, Goddess Divine!
> Inspire this crown of Your design.
> Enchant the flowers upon my wear,
> Charm my ribbons, feathers, and hair.
> Lovely Lady of beauty and grace,
> Paint Your magick upon my face.
> Mold and shape, as if were clay,
> My body to be perfect in every way.
> The scent of flowers upon my breast,
> Attracting the mate is what they do best.
> Place the sparkle within my eye,
> With wisdom, laughter and surprise.
> Satin smooth, my skin so fair,
> Shine and luster to my hair.
> Goddess reflect Your image in me,
> This is my will, So Mote It Be.

A Witch's Cleansing

Solitary Ritual (White)
by Nova

MAGICKAL INTENTION: A cleansing of the mind and the spirit.

TIME: Full Moon in May, Moon hour

TOOLS: Three white candles, Moonlight oil, and Azure incense.

INSTRUCTIONS: Anoint the three white candles with Moonlight oil. Light the candles and the incense. Stand beneath the moonlit sky and stretch your arms toward the stars. Now visualize the white illumination of the full moon filling your entire space. Feel the moon's energy sweeping over your body, cleansing your mind and spirit of anything negative. Recite the incantation. When you feel the energy fill your being, extinguish candles and know that you are cleansed.

INCANTATION:

> In this time of the growing season,
> Stand in the moonlight for this reason.
> Let the Moon's shining light,
> Purify me in its cleansing sight.
> Banish negative energy and feeling,
> Promote good health while sealing
> The promise of cleansed spirit and mind,
> Leaving negativity behind.
> By the power of three times three,
> So Mote It Be.

The Lover's Tea

Solitary Ritual (Pink)
by The Mighty Sheba

MAGICKAL INTENTION: To become smitten with love.

TIME: Full Moon in May, Venus hour

TOOLS: One pink candle, Lovers oil, Catkins incense, twenty-four raspberries, a mortar and pestle, a teakettle, a quart of water, black tea, a tea steeper, three tablespoons of sugar, and a pinch of cinnamon.

INSTRUCTIONS: Anoint the candle with the Lovers oil. Light the candle and the incense. Place the raspberries in the mortar and pestle and carefully grind them into juice and pulp. Separate the juice from the pulp and place it in the teakettle with the water and bring to a soft, continuous boil. Place the pulp and black tea in the steeper. Visualize you and your lover in a life of complete romantic bliss. As you see this image, add the sugar and cinnamon. Recite the incantation over the brew.

Allow the brew to completely cool; it is best served cold over ice. Share the tea with your lover. If the two of you happen to speak at the same time or share the same thought at the same time, your love will be sealed eternally. If this does not happen, it was not meant to be a long-lasting relationship.

INCANTATION:

> A brew of love,
> A lover's tea.
> A drink of you,
> A drink of me.
> If lovers talk,
> In harmony.
> On Lovers Moon,
> A matrimony.
> So Mote It Be.

○ ◑ ● ◐ ○

Cleansing Light

Solitary or Coven Ritual (White/Pink)
by Aquila Eagle

MAGICKAL INTENTION: To cleanse the mind, body, and spirit.

TIME: Full Moon in May, Venus hour

TOOLS: One white candle, Amulet oil, Goddess incense, a hematite, a piece of amber, a rose quartz, some holy water, and one red flannel mojo.

INSTRUCTIONS: Anoint the candle with Amulet oil. Light the candle and the incense and waft the incense smoke around the room in which you will be performing the ritual. Cleanse the three stones in holy water and sprinkle some around the room. Anoint each stone with Amulet oil.

Place the stones on the floor in a triangle big enough for you to lie down in. Place the candle at the top stone, outside of the triangle. Lie on your back with your head at the top point of the triangle and your feet at the bottom. Close your eyes and visualize the stones glowing all around you with a white light and the light forming a pyramid in and over the area where you are lying. Recite the incantation. See the white light come in through your feet and burst out of the top of your head. Carry this image with you to cleanse your mind, body and your spirit. Place the stones in the mojo and keep it in a dark place until you need to cast this spell again.

INCANTATION:

> Clear away the energies about,
> The mind, body and spirit can do without.
> The negative is what I wish,

To be gone and blessed with a kiss.
White light connects stone to stone,
Enter my being from foot to cone.
Myself is who I wish to be,
In just a moment, So Mote It Be.

○ ◐ ● ◑ ○

Unforgettable Kisses

Solitary or Coven Ritual (Pink)
by Sister Moon

MAGICKAL INTENTION: To make your kiss unforgettable.

TIME: Full Moon in May, Venus hour

TOOLS: Two pink candles, Cupid oil, Lovers incense, a brand-new Chapstick, wax paper, a mortar and pestle, three raspberries, two cherries, one strawberry, flaxseed oil, and a small jar.

INSTRUCTIONS: Anoint the candles with Cupid oil. Light the candles and the incense. Remove the Chapstick from its tube and place it on the wax paper. Crush it with the pestle. In the mortar, combine the raspberries, cherries and strawberry. Add three drops of Cupid oil and three drops of flaxseed oil. Crush until all that's left is pulp and juice. Add the juice to the Chapstick on the wax paper. Mix the juice and Chapstick well. Pass the potion through the incense and recite the incantation. Place the mixture into the small jar. When you feel the moment is appropriate for a kiss, rub a small amount on your lips!

INCANTATION:

> Within the potion of Venus bliss,
> Is the magick of a kiss.
> Stirred and crushed into the wax,
> Drops of Cupid, drops of flax.
> I conjure Venus for a spell,
> Unforgettable kiss and tell.
> Berry, cherry, berry dips,
> Irresistible are my lips.
> So Mote It Be.

○ ◐ ● ◑ ○

Jezebel's Touch

Solitary Ritual (Red)
by Crystal Ball

MAGICKAL INTENTION: To increase sexual desire.

TIME: Hare Moon in May, Venus hour

TOOLS: Two red candles, a minimum of two drams of Passion oil, Jezebel incense, your favorite massage oil, a microwave-safe earthen bowl, and chimes or a bell.

INSTRUCTIONS: Anoint the candles with Passion oil. Light the candles and the incense. Create a romantic setting for your lover. Place the massage oil in the earthen bowl. Add the rest of the Passion oil. Slightly heat the oil in the microwave so it is warm, but not hot. Recite the incantation over the oil and ring the chimes or bell. Kiss the potion to open its magick. Give your lover a sensual massage that no one on this earth can resist.

INCANTATION:
>Oil to oil, I brew this brew,
>A lover's touch when the Moon is new.
>Drops of Jezebel in this bowl,
>Bells will chime a lover's toll.
>[*Ring bell*]
>Captured love and brew of sex,
>Seducing touch within this hex.
>Resist me not in all I do,
>Arousing passion in Jezebel's brew.
>[*Ring bell*]
>So Mote It Be.
>[*Ring bell*]

NINE

The Honey Moon

🌑 🌒 🌕 🌘 🌑

> Translucent veils will crown the heads,
> Of maidens and brides the day they wed.
> Unite the hands with ribbons and twine,
> And jump the broom for love divine.

The Full Moon in June is known as The Honey Moon. This is a time to perform rituals dealing with love, the fourth chakra, unions and reunions, marriage, divining for life partners, wisdom, physical strength, endurance, inner truth, friendships, karmic debts, self-respect, conception, bounty, vacations, magickal travels, astral projection, wishing wells, any creature that can fly, and the fulfillment of dreams. This is also a time to banish hidden truths and secrets, excessiveness, and addictions of any kind.

Venus Love

Solitary Ritual (Pink)
by Indigo

MAGICKAL INTENTION: To bring about a new love.

TIME: Honey Moon, Venus hour

TOOLS: One pink candle, Venus oil, Fantasy incense, a cinnamon stick, a large piece of pink parchment, one pink rose, and a twelve-inch piece of pink string or yarn.

INSTRUCTIONS: Anoint the candle with Venus oil. Light the candle and the incense. Hold one end of the cinnamon stick in the candle flame until it glows and stub it out. On the parchment, draw a large heart with the burned end of the cinnamon stick. Inside the heart, write a description of the partner you would like to have, and the qualities you would like in a relationship. Be specific.

Take seven rose petals and roll them into the parchment with the remainder of the cinnamon stick. Visualize your true love coming to you. Once you have the mental image, put all of that energy into the scroll. Bind the spell with the pink string making three firm knots. Pass the scroll in deosil motion through the incense smoke and recite Incantation One.

Take the scroll to some swiftly flowing water and toss it in while reciting Incantation Two.

INCANTATION ONE:

> Things of pink to bring me love,
> Like a wink from above.
> Whom I search for I now bind,

And true love I will find.
So Mote It Be.

INCANTATION TWO:

Fast as the waters flow,
My true love now will show.
Bring to me the one of my dreams,
Before the next moon rises and gleams.
So Mote It Be.

The Faeries
and the Wedding Cake

Solitary Ritual (Brown)
by Sister Moon

MAGICKAL INTENTION: To become closer to your spouse and to improve your marriage.

TIME: Full Moon in June, Mercury hour

TOOLS: Two brown candles, Handfast oil, Hearthside incense, two pieces of white parchment, a wedding cake, a box of red, heart-shaped cinnamon candies, two birthday candles, and a photograph of you and your spouse. (Make sure the photograph is a Xerox or a copy and not the original.)

INSTRUCTIONS: Anoint the two candles with Handfast oil. Light the candles and the incense. On one piece of parchment, make a list of things that you would like to change about yourself, and on the other, make a list of things you would like to change about your partner. The lists must include significant things that would improve the marriage. Ask the Faery folk to aid you in these positive changes.

On the wedding cake, make a heart shape using the cinnamon candies and add the birthday candles. Place the photograph and the lists of changes on top of the cake. Light the birthday candles, recite the incantation, then blow them out.

Cut a slice of wedding cake and eat the majority of the slice but leave a smidgen for the remainder of the spell and another smidgen for the Faeries. In your garden, dig a hole by the light of the moon. Place the leftover morsels, the photograph, and the lists in the hole and bury them. Recite the incantation one more time.

INCANTATION:

> Faeries of the month of June,
> That frolic beneath the Honey Moon.
> I call upon your magick so sweet,
> To aid me in the love I seek.
> As I write upon the parchment white,
> I ask for blessings in this rite.
> Love is happiness, love is divine,
> Create the love that is to be mine.
> I feast upon the wedding cake,
> And give the Fairies their share to take.
> Love will shine by candle and fire,
> And ignite our love with great desire.
> Hearts of cinnamon, hot and red,
> Spice my life and passion bed.
> A portrait is buried beneath the moon,
> To mark the Witch that asks in June;
> For perfect love for the marriage sake,

When shared with Faeries, the wedding cake.
So Mote It Be.

○ ◑ ● ◐ ○

Satin and Lace

Coven Ritual (Red)
by Colleechee

MAGICKAL INTENTION: For tremendous physical strength.

TIME: Full Moon in June, Mars hour

TOOLS: One red candle, Mandrake oil, Mandrake incense, a seven-inch square of red satin, a needle and red thread, a piece of Low John, a piece of Dragon's Blood Reed, a pinch of basil, the shoelaces from your favorite shoes, and a potted cactus.

INSTRUCTIONS: Anoint the candle with the Mandrake oil. Light the candle and the incense. Create a pouch with the red satin by sewing together three sides. Place all the herbs in the pouch. Pass the pouch in deosil motion through the incense smoke and recite the incantation. Place one shoelace in the pouch and tie it shut with the other. Bury the pouch beneath the thriving cactus.

When you are in need of physical strength, dig up the pouch without disturbing the cactus, and lace up your shoes with the laces. Carry the pouch in your pocket.

When your time of physical endurance has passed, wait until the next full moon and pass the pouch through Mandrake incense smoke. Bury the pouch beneath the same cactus and recite the incantation again.

INCANTATION:

> Within the crimson of the fold,
> Ancient powers of strength are bold.
> Herbs will stir beneath the thorn,
> Creating energy for laces worn.
> Boost the body with greatest power,
> Mars in tune this Full Moon hour.
> Place the strength upon my feet,
> And all my powers may now compete.
> So Mote It Be.

○ ◐ ● ◑ ○

Marry Me

Solitary Ritual (Purple)
by Ivy

MAGICKAL INTENTION: To divine in a dream the person you will marry. This spell only works on single people. It will also give you an insight as to where you will live.

TIME: Hare Moon in June, Venus hour

TOOLS: One purple candle, Witch oil, Wicca incense, three teaspoons of aloe vera juice, three apple seeds, a small piece of a wedding cake, a mortar and pestle, and half a cup of water.

INSTRUCTIONS: Anoint the candle with Witch oil. Light the candle and the incense. Place the aloe juice, apple seeds and wedding cake in the mortar and pestle and grind them to a powder. Add the half-cup of water and recite the incantation three times. Drink the potion right from the mortar and immediately go to bed without talking to anyone. (You don't want your dreams influenced by others.) Pray to St. Agnes to reveal in a dream the person whom you will marry. Pay attention to details of the dream, for this will identify where you will live.

INCANTATION:

> As I lay upon this bed,
> Reveal the person that I shall wed.
> Show me the face and features fine,
> Show me the hands to tie with mine.
> Dear Saint Agnes, I call your name,
> I summon the goodness of your fame.
> Unveil the face that will be my spouse,
> My mate, my partner, my future house.
> So Mote It Be.

○ ◖ ● ◗ ○

R.E.S.P.E.C.T.

Solitary Ritual (Yellow)
by Willow

MAGICKAL INTENTION: To increase your self-respect.

TIME: The Full Moon in June, Sun hour

TOOLS: One yellow candle, Amber oil, Positive Attitude incense, one piece of yellow parchment, one piece of amber, one tiger's eye, a red flannel mojo, three carnation petals, three bay leaves, three sunflower seeds, and a cauldron.

INSTRUCTIONS: Anoint the candle with the Amber oil. Light the candle and the incense. On the yellow parchment, list nine characteristics that define self-respect. Place the stones in the mojo. Place the first petal in the mojo as you visualize yourself with the first characteristic that you listed. When you add the second petal, visualize the second characteristic that you listed. Do this for all nine characteristics as you place the petals, bay leaves, and seeds in the mojo.

Fold the parchment into a triangle and anoint each corner with the oil. Set the parchment alight using the candle flame and let it burn to ash in your cauldron. As it burns, recite the items from your list and feel each one of them growing stronger inside of you. Place the ashes in the mojo. Anoint the mojo with the Amber oil and pass it in deosil motion through the incense smoke. Carry the mojo with you at all times.

○ ◑ ● ◐ ○

Lover's Call

Solitary Ritual (Orange/Pink)
by Raiya

MAGICKAL INTENTION: To bring your true love to you.

TIME: Full Moon in June, Venus hour

TOOLS: One orange candle, Algiers oil, Be Mine incense, Dove's Blood incense, an apple, a pear, a peach, eight ounces of orange juice, a blender, a pinch of love seed, one carnelian, one emerald, and a red flannel mojo.

INSTRUCTIONS: Anoint the candle with the Algiers oil. Light the candle, combine the incenses and light them. Remove the seeds and stems from the fruit. Put the fruit and juice in the blender and blend well. Recite the incantation over the potion and drink it.

Place the seeds and stems from the fruit, the love seed, and the stones in the mojo and anoint it with the oil. Pass the mojo in de-osil motion through the incense smoke. Carry the mojo with you to attract your true love.

INCANTATION:

> Come to me true love of mine,
> Happy we'll be for all of time.
> The fruits I drink will bear the seed,
> That brings true love that I so need.
> Together, forever, my lover and friend,
> For a love so pure will never end.
> The spell is cast and Fate will see,
> My one and only soon come to me.
> So Mote It Be.

○ ◐ ● ◑ ○

Postdated Checks

Solitary Ritual (White/Pink)
by Journey

MAGICKAL INTENTION: To address karmic debt with love and light.

TIME: Full Moon in June, Jupiter hour

TOOLS: One pink candle, one white candle, Moonlight oil, Beloved incense, one moonstone, one teaspoon of dried sage, a mortar and pestle, one personal check, a cauldron, consecrated water, and one sage leaf.

INSTRUCTIONS: Anoint both candles with the Moonlight oil. Light the candles and the incense. Anoint the moonstone with the oil. Place the dried sage in the mortar and pestle and grind it. Fill out your check as follows:

> *Date:* The date of the ritual
> *Pay to the order of:* Karmic Debt
> *Dollar amount:* $All
> *Write on the amount line:* Live, learn, love and grow
> *Memo:* truth and peace

Sign the check and ignite it with the flame of the pink candle. Add the sage and burn the check and leaf together in the cauldron. Add the consecrated water and stir the mixture with the sage leaf in deosil motion thirteen times, while reciting the incantation twice.

Pour the mixture onto the earth and recite the incantation one final time.

INCANTATION:

> Karmic debt is a wonderful thing,
> Through this process my soul takes wings.
> The postdated check is now due,
> This is the time to start anew.
> To live and learn,
> And to love and grow.
> Till truth and peace,
> Is all that I know.
> So Mote It Be.

TEN
Litha

The sun will bless the longest day,
And Witches gather herbs and play.
Stocking the cupboards with magick delight,
Savoring the warmth of midsummer's night.

Litha is on June 21 or 22 and is a minor Sabbat. It is also known as Midsummer's Day, and is also the longest day of the year. This is a time to perform rituals dealing with psychic ability, garden magick, pregnancy, children, magickal herbs, familiars and other pets, talismans and amulets, attraction of all kinds, romance, unions, marriages, weddings, protection, physical and emotional strength, and rituals that honor parents and grandparents.

Midsummer Night's Dream

Solitary or Coven Ritual (Purple)
by Sister Moon

MAGICKAL INTENTION: To attract your future mate.

TIME: June 21 or 22, Venus hour

TOOLS: One orange candle, White Solstice oil, White Solstice incense, red wine, a chalice, fresh red and pink roses, a ball of white yarn, a y-shaped branch from a fruit-bearing tree, a variety of beads, laces, ribbons, and wild flowers, and a pillow.

INSTRUCTIONS: Anoint the candle with White Solstice oil. Light the candle and the incense. Pour the red wine into the chalice and add the petals.

Wind the yarn around the y-shaped branch until it's covered. Place loops on the ends so it can be hung. Braid the long side of the branch in a decorative manner using the laces and ribbons. Add the beads and wildflowers to make it attractive.

Visualize the qualities you would like your mate to have. When you have finished, hang the branch from a tree. Close your eyes and drink from the chalice and make one wish in regard to your mate.

Lie on your back with the pillow to cushion your head and close your eyes again. Feel the spell attracting your mate. Recite the incantation. Then gaze at the stars above you. A falling star will confirm the speed of your spell.

INCANTATION:

>Midsummer's night dream within a spell,
>Weave a talisman to compel.
>I drink from the chalice of love and rose,

My answer revealed when my eyes are closed.
So Mote It Be.

○ ◐ ● ◑ ○

The Witching Wreath

Solitary or Coven (Rainbow magick)
by Lyra

MAGICKAL INTENTION: To empower herbs for magickal use.

TIME: June 21 or 22, Venus hour

TOOLS: One blue candle, Mediterranean Magick oil, Witching Well incense, a twelve-inch natural grapevine wreath, twenty-seven nine-inch pieces of ribbon in all the colors of the rainbow, fresh-picked herbs with stems, several naturally fallen feathers from friendly fowls, and bright red and yellow ribbons to tie the feathers to the wreath.

INSTRUCTIONS: Anoint the candle with Mediterranean Magick oil. Light the candle and the incense. Thread the rainbow colored ribbons through the wreath and place one kind of herb in the center and tie the ribbon into a bow. Continue threading the ribbon and tying the different herbs onto the wreath. Attach the feathers with the red and yellow ribbons so they hang down in the center of the wreath. Pass the wreath in deosil motion through the incense smoke and recite the incantation.

Hang the wreath in your kitchen to dry by a gentle breeze. Use the herbs for those extra-special recipes that need magickal ingredients. Leave the ribbons intact so you can refill the wreath next summer with fresh herbs.

INCANTATION:

> Bless this wreath so gay and bright,
> With herbs that I picked with delight.
> To hold their powers until I might,
> Infuse the potions that are just right.
> Bring health and happiness,
> With all their strength.
> To aid in matters both large and small,
> Bless this wreath, herbs, feathers and all.
> So Mote It Be.

○ ◑ ● ◐ ○

Hercule's Help

Solitary or Coven Ritual (Red)
by Crystal Ball

MAGICKAL INTENTION: For emotional strength.

TIME: June 21 or 22, Mars hour

TOOLS: One red candle, Eucalyptus oil, Mandrake incense, a brownie mix, a pan in which to cook the brownies, one red carnation, a quarter-cup of walnuts, and a quarter-cup of pine nuts.

INSTRUCTIONS: Anoint the candle with Eucalyptus oil. Light the candle and the incense. Make the brownie mix according to directions. Before the mixture is poured into the baking pan, tear petals

from the red carnation and place them in the mixture (not too many, a few will do). Add the walnuts and pine nuts. Stir well. Recite the incantation and stir in deosil motion thirteen times. Bake as directed. The brownies will give you the emotional strength you are seeking.

INCANTATION:

> With the blend of nuts of pine,
> I create the strength I now call mine.
> Add the petal of this red flower,
> I gain the strength of emotional power.
> I call upon Hercules to help this potion,
> Thirteen turns in deosil motion.
> I once was weak, but now I'm strong,
> Hercules helps me all day long.
> So Mote It Be.

○ ◑ ● ◑ ○

Star Charms

Solitary or Coven Ritual (White/Blue)
by Luna

MAGICKAL INTENTION: To create an amulet of protection for a Witch or Warlock.

TIME: June 21 or 22, Saturn hour

TOOLS: Five white candles, Protection oil, about two cups of sea salt or regular salt, Amulet incense, and an amulet that is suspended by a chain.

INSTRUCTIONS: Anoint the five candles with the Protection oil. Using the salt, outline a large pentagram. Place a white candle at each point of the pentagram. Light the incense. Pass the amulet in deosil motion through the incense smoke. Concentrate on this amulet and the protection it provides. Place the amulet in the center of the salted pentagram. Recite the incantation once and then light the candle that is directly to the right of the amulet. Repeat this action until all five candles are lit. Allow the magick to be absorbed into the amulet. When it is done, seal the amulet with Protection oil.

INCANTATION:

On the longest day of the year,
Witches and Warlocks have no fear.
Love, beauty, passions, and energy,
The fire festivals are near.
With Litha, a powerful amulet is born.
That can protect from evil,
Each time it is worn.
A magickal charm that wards off all harm
So Mote It Be.

Growing Rocks

Solitary or Coven Ritual (Green)
by Sister Moon

MAGICKAL INTENTION: To make a garden flourish with growth.

TIME: June 21 or 22, Jupiter hour

TOOLS: Three green candles, Fertility oil, Goddess incense, a large amount of rich, tilled soil for the garden, a large container to mix in, small pinches of lavender seeds, spearmint seeds, marigold seeds, and sweetpea seeds, one malachite, one aventurine, one piece of coral, and a large container of water.

INSTRUCTIONS: Anoint the candle with Fertility oil. Light the candle and the incense. Place the rich soil in the large container. Using your hands, mix in the seeds and recite incantation. Scatter the soil in your garden.

Place the stones in your garden in a pyramid shape. Recite the incantation again and water your garden.

If the seeds take, do not pull out or destroy the plants; allow them to live in your garden. This will ensure the growth of all your other plants. Your garden will flourish with abundance.

INCANTATION:

> Enchantment of this earth so brown,
> Rich and plentiful is the ground.
> Make this garden grow and flourish,
> With careful magick it is nourished.
> Sew in the seeds of herb and flower,
> Place the stones to boost the power.
> Gracious Goddess remove all blocks,
> And empower this garden of growing
>   rocks.
> So Mote It Be.

○ ◐ ● ◑ ○

Thank You

Solitary or Coven Ritual (Gold/Purple)
by Raiya

MAGICKAL INTENTION: A ritual to honor grandparents.

TIME: June 21 or 22, Moon hour

TOOLS: One large, gold candle, Magick incense, Witch oil, a pinch each of eucalyptus, gardenia, and moonwort, the peeling from a completely dried cucumber, three lemon seeds, one photograph of your grandparents, two pieces of gold fabric measuring the same size as your photograph plus one-third of an inch more on all sides, purple thread, a needle, and four naturally fallen willow branches approximately same size as your photograph (this will create your frame).

INSTRUCTIONS: Anoint the candle with Witch oil. Light the candle and the incense. Combine the herbs, seeds, and peel in your hand. As you do this, concentrate on pure white energy flowing through you and into the herb mixture. Remember the laughter, love, and all the good times you have shared with the people in the photograph. When you feel you have charged the herb mixture with enough energy, set them aside. Place both pieces of fabric right-side together. Sew up three of the sides with a quarter-inch seam. Turn the pouch right-side out. Place the herbs into the pouch and sew up the last seam. As you sew, recite the incantation. Place one willow branch on one side of the fabric and gently sew the branch to the material. Do this with each side and carefully slip the photograph into its new frame. Recite the incantation again.

Anoint each corner of the frame with Witch oil. Place the framed picture anywhere in your home. Each time you look at it, you are surrounding your beloved grandparents in pure white energy.

INCANTATION:
> Thank you for your love and light,
> I honor you this Litha night.
> Wisdom, knowledge, instilled in me,
> Without you, I would never be.
> In each stitch, I place my love,
> With blessings from the Guardians above.
> I honor you parents of love so grand,
> And cherish your memory as I stand.
> So Mote It Be.

○ ◐ ● ◑ ○

Enchanted Familiars

Solitary or Coven Ritual (Purple)
by Ambrosia

MAGICKAL INTENTION: To increase a familiar's ability to aid the Witch in spell casting.

TIME: June 21 or 22, Moon hour

TOOLS: One purple candle, Witch oil, Magick incense, and your familiar.

INSTRUCTIONS: Anoint the candle with Witch oil. Light the candle and the incense. While reciting the incantation, draw a pentagram on the forehead of the familiar with Witch oil. Visualize your familiar gaining power and understanding its position in aiding you in spells.

INCANTATION:

>Invoke the elements of the magickal star,
>To magnify the mind's vision far.
>Earth, Water, Fire, Air,
>When using magick have a care.
>Aid in spell casting on this night,
>Increasing awareness and sight.
>Enhance thought to attain clairvoyance,
>Leaving not a thing to chance.
>So Mote It Be.

ELEVEN
The Festive Moon

Magickal gardens and midsummer's faeries,
Frolic and laughter inspires the merry.
To dance in the gardens bare-breasted and free,
Unleashing the Moon playing Festive with me.

The Full Moon in July is known as The Festive Moon. This is a time to perform rituals dealing with celebrations in general, peace, protection in general, harmony, marriage, life partners, freedom, free will, choices, karmic connections, intuition, friendships, fertility of animals, world negotiations, contracts, any form of sea life, increase of psychic abilities, and chemistry on all levels. It is also a time to banish sterility, stalemates, and unresolved issues.

The Celebration of Marriage

Partners' Ritual (Brown)
by Indigo

MAGICKAL INTENTION: To celebrate a happy union. Both parties must be present.

TIME: Full Moon in July, Venus hour

TOOLS: One brown candle, Marriage Mind oil, Cedarwood incense, a half cup of each of the following: chopped apples, bananas, cherries, peaches, raspberries, and pears, the juice of one lime, one cup of white sugar, one large bowl, one large spoon, two small bowls, a two foot piece of brown, pink, and blue ribbons, and one daisy, one gardenia, and one rose.

INSTRUCTIONS: With your partner, anoint the candle with the oil. Light the candle and the incense. Mix the fruit pieces, lime juice and sugar in the large bowl. Stir the brew well with the large spoon. With your partner, recite the incantation over the brew. Dish the fruit into the two small bowls. Sit with your partner and braid the pieces of ribbon together. With each pass of the ribbon, take turns telling each other the positive things about your marriage. Talk about the things you enjoy and the things that you would like to change in your relationship. Express the love that you feel for each other.

When the braid is completed, tie a knot in both ends of the ribbons. Now tie the ribbons around the stems of the flowers and leave them on the table. Eat the fruits to strengthen your marriage and your love for each other. When you are done, hang the flowers in the house to remind you of your love.

INCANTATION:

> Fruits of nature,
> Bring love and nurture.
> Bless our marriage vows,
> Fruits of nature.
> Bring love and nurture.
> Strengthen our marriage now,
> Fruits of nature.
> Bring love and nurture,
> Celebrate our love now.
> This is our will,
> So Mote It Be.

Thirteen Treasures

Coven Ritual (Brown)
by Sister Moon

MAGICKAL INTENTION: To complete karmic debts.

TIME: Full Moon in July, Moon hour

TOOLS: One brown candle, one green candle, one purple candle, Jade oil, Covenstead incense, Seven Powers incense, one each of the following magickal stones: clear quartz, blue turquoise, rose quartz, yellow leopard, ruby in matrix, coral, green tourmaline, purple fluorite, hematite, black obsidian, pyrite, tiger's eye and a banded amthethyst, a scrying bowl, and three cups of water.

INSTRUCTIONS: Anoint all of the candles with Jade oil. Combine the Covenstead incense with the Seven Powers incense. Light the candles and the incense. Place the thirteen magickal stones into the scrying bowl. Add the water. Recite the incantation, then close your eyes. Pull one stone from the scrying bowl. Commit the stone to memory, replace it, and pass the scrying bowl to the next member.

Read the karmic duty of that stone below. It is up to you to resolve this debt within one moon's cycle.

INCANTATION:

> Thirteen treasures of the Earth,
> I assume my debt and my worth.
> Homage is paid to the Goddess serene,
> And for the bounty of all that is green.
> The debt of lives that were of past,
> Have karmic impressions within the glass.
> I choose to pay the debt I owe,
> Freely and gladly with waters flow.
> Life of past, I reach your stone,
> I release the debt of life unknown.
> Karmic score I settle with pride,
> I resolve this issue in one moon's stride.
> So Mote It Be.

THE THIRTEEN STONES:

1. *Clear Quartz:* In a past lifetime, you witnessed a group of people being cruel to animals. You did nothing to stop them. It is your duty to repair the wrongdoings of these people. You must do an extra kind deed for an animal or animals that you do not even know. Do this task within one moon's cycle.

2. *Blue Turquoise:* In a past lifetime, you belonged to a tribe of

Native Americans. There were no white people upon your land. A great tree was planted to symbolize strength, prosperity, endurance, and the importance of great family. It is your task to plant a great tree with a turquoise stone beneath it to represent these qualities. You must complete this within one moon's cycle.

3. *Rose Quartz:* In a past lifetime, you professed your love to someone that you trusted and it was rejected. You were so devastated by this that you ended your own life. It is your debt to heal your rejection and to find strength enough to overcome what others have done to you. Your debt is to write a spell to mend a broken heart and cast it for someone who is heartbroken. You must do this task within one moon's cycle.

4. *Yellow Leopard:* In a past lifetime, you were the victim of a disease that took your life painfully and swiftly. Hundreds of people died from this awful disease. In your state of passing, you envisioned that you were a bird flying off to heaven. This gave you peace. It is your debt to help the wild birds build a safe home for the upcoming winter. You must complete this task in one moon's cycle.

5. *Ruby in Matrix:* In a past lifetime, you lived in Europe and were a wealthy clothing merchant. You sold only the finest clothing to the most elite customers. You did not associate with people of lesser means. It is your debt to clothe the poor. You must donate any extra clothing that you no longer need to a worthy charity of your choice. You must do this in one moon's cycle.

6. *Coral:* In a past lifetime, you were a child who died of starvation. It is your debt to feed a hungry child or children whom you do not already know. Do this by donating food items or money to purchase food to any starving child in the world. You must complete this task within one moon's cycle.

7. *Green Tourmaline:* In a past lifetime, you were an experienced healer. You healed many sick people; the only person you lost was someone with whom you were close. You felt responsible that you were unable to heal this special person. It is your debt to pray for the sick and suffering every day for one moon's cycle.

8. *Purple Fluorite:* In a past lifetime, you lived in an ancient land and you were a noble prophet for a king. You foretold of battles, love, inventions, and events that pertained to the king's life and enjoyment. It is your task to do a reading that foretells one year of the life for an individual you feel you owe something to. You must complete this task within one moon's cycle.

9. *Hematite:* In a past lifetime, you were burned alive for being a Witch. To release the negativity of the fire, you must make three magick candles. Each candle is to be given to three different Witches. All candles must be made with the intent of protection. You must do this task within one moon's cycle.

10. *Black Obsidian:* In a past lifetime, you were a child who never knew of birthdays, Christmas, or gift giving. It is your debt to purchase something special for an underprivileged child. Wrap it in pretty paper and give it to this child for absolutely no reason whatsoever. You must complete this task within one moon's cycle.

11. *Pyrite:* In a past lifetime, you were a person who worked in caves and mines, digging every day for the precious gold that the Earth held deep within it. You spent the majority of your time in the dark dampness of the earth. Your debt is to create a chest of earthly treasures and to share it with people who live in darkness. You must complete this task within one moon's cycle.

12. *Tiger's Eye:* In a past lifetime, you were a sailor on the seas. Even though you had seen many different lands, the sea was the only real home that you knew. Your debt is to pay homage to water. Contribute time or money to the whales, dolphins, or any seafaring organization that will help this planet. You must do this task within one moon's cycle.

13. *Banded Amethyst:* In a past lifetime, your life was spared by a Good Samaritan who defended you when you were attacked by thieves. As a result, the Samaritan lost her life. As you held the dying stranger in your arms, her only request was that you do something kind for someone you don't even know. It is your task to compete this debt within one moon's cycle.

○ ◐ ● ◑ ○

World Peace

Solitary or Coven Ritual (Rainbow Magick)
by Aquila Eagle

MAGICKAL INTENTION: To end war and promote peace on earth.

TIME: Full Moon in July, Sun hour

TOOLS: One blue candle, Special Favors and Lotus oils, Criss Cross, Purity, Angel Wings, Deosil, and Blessed Be incenses, a pinch each of carob, lemon, pascalite, and safflower, a mortar and pestle, and a mojo bag for each participant.

INSTRUCTIONS: Anoint the candle with Lotus and Special Favors oils. Light the candle. Add a small portion of each incense into the burner and light the mixture. Combine all of the herbs in the mortar. Pass the mortar and pestle through the incense smoke.

Allow the incense to burn out. After it has completely cooled, combine it with the herbs in the mortar. Place the mixture into the mojos. Take the mojos to a large body of water. Recite the incantation while visualizing peace on earth. Release the mixture from each mojo into the water and visualize the potion reaching every country in the world.

INCANTATION:

> Angels all around us, wherever we may be,
> The United States, Afghanistan and all countries.
> In this water we send with you,
> The peace of all countries that will be true.
> Around the world, please hear this call,
> To guide and heal us one and all.
> Protect us from each other's harm,
> Reverse and rid bad energies until they are gone.
> Calm our hearts and our minds,
> Bring peace and love to every kind.
> All around our world will be,
> Filled with happiness, peace and harmony.
> Heal us from our core within,
> So we may not judge one another again.
> Forgive us our sins and protect our hearts,
> From fears we have in various parts.
> Religion, politics, whatever may be,
> Heal and protect us from each other,
> So Mote It Be.

○ ◑ ● ◐ ○

Forever Friends

Solitary or Coven Ritual (Pink)
by Daughter of Dragons

MAGICKAL INTENTION: For lasting friendships. This spell is so strong that it is rumored to last for eternity.

TIME: Full Moon in July, Mercury hour

TOOLS: Two pink candles, Friendship oil, Friendship incense, two very small pictures of the two of you together, and two lockets with chains.

INSTRUCTIONS: Anoint the candles with Friendship oil. Light the candles and the incense. Cut the pictures to fit into each locket. Each person should write her name on the back of each picture. Place the pictures in the lockets and close them. Anoint the back of the locket with Friendship oil. Pass the lockets in deosil motion through the incense smoke while reciting the incantation. Place the lockets around your necks. Keep the locket in a safe place when you are not wearing it. The spell is sealed eternally.

INCANTATION:

> Two pink candles all aglow,
> Dancing flames, to and fro.
> Like the candles, so are we,
> Friends for now and always be.
> I wear your face over my heart,
> From this day we'll never part.
> From start of day till night does end,
> We will always be best of friends.
> So Mote It Be.

○ ◐ ● ◑ ○

U B Fun at the BBQ

Solitary Ritual (Yellow)
by Sister Moon

MAGICKAL INTENTION: To be the life of the party. This spells works very well for the shy and inhibited.

TIME: Full Moon in July, Mercury hour

TOOLS: Two large yellow candles, two large orange candles, Merry Meet oil, Friendship incense, a lemon, a punch bowl, crackers and cheese, a cup of cooked mushrooms, a jar of pimentos, Cherry 7-Up, and Hawaiian Punch.

INSTRUCTIONS: Anoint all four candles with Merry Meet oil. Light the candles and the incense. Rub the inside of the punch bowl with the half of the lemon, and recite the incantation twice. Slice the cheese and put it on the crackers. Recite the incantation over the mushrooms and pimentos and add them to the cheese and crackers. Pass the punch bowl and the snack you've made through the incense smoke. Recite the incantation one last time.

Pour the Cherry 7-Up and the Hawaiian Punch into punch bowl. Slice the remaining lemon half and hang the slices on the sides of the punch bowl. Leave the candles lit throughout the party.

INCANTATION:
> I cast the spell for my pleasure,
> Sipping brew with guests of measure.
> Laughter gathers wherever I stand,
> For I'm on stage and you're my fans.

Applause I seek and I shall receive,
All the attention that I need.
Party of parties, for I am the light,
All of your smiles are my delight.
So Mote It Be.

○ ◑ ● ◑ ○

Tingles

Solitary Ritual (Orange/Pink)
by Queen of the Meadow

MAGICKAL INTENTION: To increase your chemistry with friends and make good friendships.

TIME: Full Moon in July, Moon hour

TOOLS: One large orange candle, Bewitching oil, Friendship incense, one piece of turquoise, one hematite, one tiger's eye (make sure all the stones are similar in size and shape), and one red flannel mojo.

INSTRUCTIONS: Anoint the candle with the Bewitching oil. Light the candle and the incense. Place all the stones in the red flannel mojo. Pass the mojo in deosil motion through the incense smoke and recite the incantation.

When having a friend over, bring out the mojo, show her the stones and explain which one is which. Then put them back in the bag. Have your friend close her eyes and pick a stone using her power hand. See if she can identify which stone she is holding without opening her eyes. Do this for all three stones. If she identifies all three stones correctly, tingles will race up your spine, and you will know this is a true and close friendship. If she identifies two stones correctly, this will be a fine friendship. If she identifies one stone correctly, she is just an acquaintance. If she doesn't identify any of the stones correctly, this is not a good friendship at all.

INCANTATION:

> Stones of three,
> Blind man draws.
> Reveal to me,
> The friends I call.
> Three of three,
> More than mingle,
> Friends for life,
> Magick tingles.
> Two be right,
> One be wrong,
> Distant light,
> Sings the song.
> One precise,
> Two be missed,
> Smile twice,
> Acquaintances.
> Stones of nil,
> Marks the score.
> Empty the till,
> Friends no more.
> So Mote It Be.

○ ◐ ● ◑ ○

The Magickal Cupboard

Solitary Ritual (Purple)
by Raven

MAGICKAL INTENTION: To clean and empower the cupboard in which you store your magickal tools.

TIME: Full Moon in July, Moon hour

TOOLS: One purple candle, Seven Powers oil, Witch incense, a two-gallon bucket, one gallon of clean, warm water, one teaspoon of vinegar, one teaspoon of salt, three tablespoons of the appropriate cleaner for your cupboard (if your cupboard is wood, use a fine wood oil, if it is plastic or glass, use a glass cleaner) one tablespoon of eucalyptus, one teaspoon of rubbing alcohol, and two paper towels.

INSTRUCTIONS: Anoint the candle with Seven Powers oil. Light the candle and the incense. Fill the bucket with the water. Add the next five ingredients (vinegar through alcohol) and recite the incantation over the mixture. Clean all of the cupboards using one paper towel to wash and one paper towel to dry.

INCANTATION:
> Festive Moon empower and clean,
> All the magick that I redeem.
> Revitalize my source and my tools,
> To ensure the power and the rules.
> Within this brew, I shall cleanse,
> All ingredients of magickal blends.
> Bless their storage and keep them well,
> When used by me within my spells.
> So Mote It Be.

TWELVE

Lammas

Summon the faeries on Llamas eve,
To write in grimoires the spells we weave.
Protect the shadows in auras of blue,
Safeguard the Crones and the Wizards, too.

Lammas is on August 1 and is a major Sabbat. This is a time to perform rituals dealing with the Goddess and God, faeries, completion, bounty, cleansing the home, weather magick, crops, foods, poppets, Crones and Wizards, loneliness, unattached people who desire relationships, solidifying family members, the earth and the environment, promises, contracts, books, legalities, and knowledge.

Praise the Bounty

Coven Ritual (White)
by Ivy

MAGICKAL INTENTION: To honor the Goddess and God for the bounty of the first harvest by making a poppet.

TIME: August 1, Jupiter hour

TOOLS: One white candle, White Solstice oil, White Solstice incense, and enough of the following ingredients for the entire Coven: apples, peaches, grapes, unsliced bread, an assortment of dried fruits, flowers, vegetable seeds, four or five ears of corn with the husks left on for each participant, one crabapple for each participant, one spool of kite string, and one jar of peanut butter.

INSTRUCTIONS: Cast a full circle. Anoint the candle with the White Solstice oil. Light the candle and the incense. Each participant should follow the instructions to create a poppet.

Shuck the corn and lay out the cornhusks. Place a crabapple in the center of a husk and wrap it around, tying it securely with the kite string. This will be the head. Add another husk for the body. Tie off the top and bottom of the body husk and stuff it with corn, bread, seeds, and fruits.

To make the arms and legs, roll a piece of husk lengthwise and pass it through the body at the bottom for the legs and at the top for the arms. Use the peanut butter as your glue, and decorate your poppet with flowers and any remaining seeds or dried fruit.

When your poppet is complete, anoint the head, hands, and feet with White Solstice oil and recite the incantation. When the spell has been cast, take your poppet to a grove of trees, a forest, a field, or even a garden. Leave it there as a love offering to the Goddess and God for the wonderful bounty that They have given us.

INCANTATION:

> Little poppet made of corn,
> Fruits of earth do adorn.
> Grown from the ground with care and love,
> Watched by the spirits from above.
> Gathered from the bountiful harvest,
> From the fields and to the forest.
> To the mighty Goddess and God that be,
> With thanks we offer this bounty to thee.
> This is my will, So Mote It Be.

The Bountiful Harvest

Solitary or Coven Ritual (Green/Gold)
by Lyra

MAGICKAL INTENTION: To bless the gardens and fields before the harvest.

TIME: August 1, the Sunrise hour

TOOLS: One large green candle, Helping Hand oil, Cleomay incense, small handfuls of dried corn, wheat, and oats, and a mortar and pestle.

INSTRUCTIONS: Anoint the candle with Helping Hand oil. Light the candle and the incense. Place the dried grains in the mortar and grind into a powder with the pestle. Pass the mortar through the incense smoke and recite Incantation One. Divide the powdered grains into four different heaps and offer them the four Quadrants. Recite Incantation Two over each of the mounds, and allow the wind to scatter them.

INCANTATION ONE:

> We grind these grains,
> With prayers and hopes,
> That they will scatter,
> In the winds of the Hosts.
> May they bless this harvest,
> We tendered with care,
> To nourish our bodies,
> Throughout the year.
> So Mote It Be.

INCANTATION TWO:

> We harvest these plants with love and care,
> And thank the Earth who let them bear.
> These fruits and grains so rich and ripe,
> To grace our table throughout the nights.
> So Mote It Be.

The Bread Basket

Coven Ritual (Brown)
by Sister Moon

MAGICKAL INTENTION: To share the bounty.

TIME: August 1, Sun hour

TOOLS: A brown candle for each participant, White Solstice oil, White Solstice incense, a set of rune stones, a very large basket, three different types of bread, chalices and wine, butter and jam, all kinds of colorful beads, bells, and ribbons in the following colors: white, blue, pink, red, orange, yellow, gold, brown, light green, dark green, light purple, and dark purple.

INSTRUCTIONS: Anoint the candles with the oil. Light the candles and the incense. Place the runes upside-down in the basket. Each participant draws a rune. Look below and find the colors and meaning for each rune. Make a braid of the appropriate three colors with the ribbons, using the beads and bells as decorations. When all of the braids are finished, attach them to or weave them into the basket.

All participants join hands and recite the incantation. Place the bread into the basket and pour the wine. Everyone eats at least one piece of bread and toasts the rune that will affect his or her life.

INCANTATION:
> Lammas basket for many breads,
> Woven by Witches with a dozen threads.
> Magick flowing from bells and braids,
> Ensuring bounty for those whom made,
> The Lammas day basket for bountiful bread.
> So Mote It Be.

THE RUNES:
Fehu: Wealth; dark green, light green, and gold.
Uruz: Power; dark purple, light purple, and white.
Ansuz: Love; pink, red, and white.
Raido: Travel; yellow, green, and white.

Kano: Intelligence; yellow, gold, and white.

Gebo: Gifts; pink, white, and yellow.

Wunjo: Reward; blue, purple, and pink.

Jera: Harvest; green, brown, and white.

Eihwaz: Strength; purple, brown, and yellow.

Perth: Abundance; green, orange, and white.

Algiz: Protection; blue, purple, and white.

Teiwaz: Truth; yellow, purple, and white.

Berkana: Beauty; pink, white, and gold.

Ehwaz: Movement; orange, green, and white.

Mannaz: Inspiration; purple, white, and gold.

Laguz: Dreams; blue, purple, and green.

Inguz: Family; brown, blue, and pink.

Dagaz: Accomplishment; brown, white, and gold.

Othila: Karma; red, blue, and yellow.

○ ◑ ● ◑ ○

Peaceful Dreams

Solitary Ritual (White/Blue)
by Leebrah

MAGICKAL INTENTION: To cleanse the bedroom with the magick of new curtains.

TIME: August 1, any hour

TOOLS: One white candle, oils of Moonlight, Dream, Lotus, and Peace, Drive Away Evil and Azure incenses, clean blue and white fabric, a sewing machine, thread, an earthen bowl, and the following herbs: chamomile, lettuce, yerba santa, cypress, mahogany, bamboo, and hydrangea.

INSTRUCTIONS: Anoint the white candle with the combination of oils. Light the candle and the incenses.

Using the fabric and the sewing machine, make curtains to fit the bedroom window. Leave at least one inch of hemline open end to end. Combine all of the herbs with two drops of each oil in the earthen bowl and mix well. Sprinkle the mixture into the hemline of the curtains making sure that the potion is distributed evenly and sew the hemline closed. Pass the curtains in deosil motion through the incense smoke. Recite the incantation.

When you wash the curtains, undo the hemline and remove the herbs. You can repeat this spell any time of the year.

INCANTATION:

> During all hours of the day,
> Evil will stay at bay.
> I use these herbs of various kinds,
> To bring a clearing to my mind.
> As I sleep no fear will come,
> Only blessings for this one.
> This room is cleansed from wall
>   to wall,
> All around me, I will not fall.
> Beauty, protection, wishes and love,
> All come about with help from above.
> Calmness in my heart and mind,
> For restful sleep is what I find.
> The cleansing of this room will bring,
> A night full of peaceful dreams.
> I cast this spell out you see,
> This is my will, So Mote It Be.

○ ◑ ● ◐ ○

Faeries Harvest

Solitary or Coven Ritual (Yellow)
by Ambrosia

MAGICKAL INTENTION: To invite the faeries to join in a ritual of thanksgiving for the harvest.

TIME: August 1, Sun hour

TOOLS: One yellow candle, White Solstice oil, White Solstice incense, an athame, and a loaf of homemade bread.

INSTRUCTIONS: Anoint the candle with White Solstice oil. Light the candle and the incense. With the athame, draw a pentagram over the bread, and recite the incantation. Slice the bread and break one slice into several small pieces for the faeries.

INCANTATION:
>As the faeries flit to and fro,
>A celebration of Lammas to show,
>Thanks for the bountiful harvest this year,
>By consumption of bread, let the Goddess hear.
>With the aid of a magickal star,
>To shout heartfelt thanks loud and far,
>Under the Lammas moon, "thanks" we say,
>While a festival of faeries is underway.
>So Mote It Be.

○ ◑ ● ◐ ○

Purple Stones

Coven Ritual (Purple)
by Sister Moon

MAGICKAL INTENTION: A ritual to honor the Crones and Wizards.

TIME: August 1, Sun hour

TOOLS: One large purple candle for each Crone or Wizard that is present, Witch oil, Witch incense, white silk carnations, a wreath (to use as a headpiece) made of twigs or other natual materials, thirteen amethysts, dried babies' breath, a purple pillow, a hot glue gun, and white, purple, and gold ribbons.

INSTRUCTIONS: Anoint the candles with the oil. Light the candles and the incense. Adorn the wreath with the white carnations. Glue the amethysts to the carnations. If the wearer is a Crone, tie the ribbons so they flow down from the back. The crown should be tasteful and beautiful.

Pass the crown through the incense smoke and anoint it with the oil. Recite the incantation.

When the Coven gathers, place the crown in the center of the magick circle. The High Priestess holds the crown on the pillow and recites the incantation. Then she kneels before the Crone and then places the crown on the Crone's head. (If there is more than one Crone or Wizard being honored, there should be a purple pillow to hold each crown.)

INCANTATION:

> Stones of purple and stones of power,
> Amethyst invoked this Witching hour.

Honor bestowed upon the Crone,
Of Wiccan crowns of purple stones.
We honor your presence and your power,
Amethyst invoked this Witching hour.
Bless this Witch that wears the crown,
Crones and Wizards draw the Moon down.
Stones of purple and stones of power,
Amethyst invoked this Witching hour.
We gather together to honor your presence,
To entwine your magick and your essence.
Stones of purple and stones of power,
Amethyst invoked this Witching hour.
So Mote It Be.

○ ◑ ● ◑ ○

Blind Justice

Solitary or Coven Ritual (Purple)
by Poseidon

MAGICKAL INTENTION: To allow the truth be told in a legal matter. This spell is potent for one full year. (If for any reason you have done something you know to be wrong, don't cast this spell.)

TIME: August 1, Saturn hour

TOOLS: One gold candle, one gray candle, one purple candle, Just Judge oil and incense, three hematites, three pigeon feathers, a bell small enough to conceal in your pocket, and a red flannel mojo.

INSTRUCTIONS: Anoint all three candles with the oil. Light the candles and the incense. Anoint all three stones with the oil. Visualize a judge smiling favorably upon you. See the judge remove a blindfold from her or his eyes. See yourself returning the judge's smile.

Place the stone, feathers, and bell in the mojo and seal it. Pass the mojo in deosil motion through the incense smoke. Recite the incantation.

Store in a dark, quiet place. If you need to go to court, place the mojo in your left pocket. Place your hand in your pocket and move the items in the pouch around while pleading your case. The Judge will hear what you have to say and smile upon you.

INCANTATION:
>Winged courier now takes flight,
>Aid me in my legal plight.
>Press the feathers against the stone,
>Ring the bell and truth be known.
>Habeas corpus in this court,
>Grant me favor of legal sport.
>Release the magick and judge be just,
>Hear my plea and statement you trust.
>So Mote It Be.

THIRTEEN

The Poet's Moon

From novice to Crone, a Witch will fly,
To paint a sunset in the sky.
To capture the person who writes the tune,
That bewitches the heart on Poet's Moon.

The Full Moon in August is known as The Poet's Moon. This is a time to perform rituals dealing with writing and creating new spells, the fifth chakra, increasing psychic skills and perfecting magickal techniques on all levels, Wiccanings, Croning rituals, religious freedom, healing of the soul, creating perfumes, oils, and incenses, faery magick, protecting the earth and its resources, playing games of skills or chance, protection of animals, fantasies, expansion of the imagination, and romantic skills. It is also a time to banish all obstacles, negative imagery, and bad memories.

Heaven's Power

Coven Ritual (Purple)
by Ariel

MAGICKAL INTENTION: To increase your psychic abilities. (You must have at least eight members in your Coven for this ritual.

TIME: Full Moon in August, Jupiter hour.

TOOLS: One purple candle, Blue Moon oil, Summer Rain incense, a fresh coconut divided so that each participant has a piece, a handful of chives, fresh mushrooms, a large earthen bowl, and a large red flannel mojo for each participant.

INSTRUCTIONS: Anoint the candle with Blue Moon oil. Light the candle and the incense. Place all ingredients into the earthen bowl. Recite Incantation One and pass the bowl in deosil motion through the incense smoke.

Put a piece of coconut shell, some chives, and some mushrooms into each mojo. Pass each mojo in deosil motion through the incense smoke and recite Incantation Two. Bury the mojos deep into the earth near an outdoor altar and seal the magick by pouring the wax from the purple candle into the hole.

INCANTATION ONE:

> When night has pulled the shades down tight,
> And the Moon rides high and full,
> We gather 'round the things we need,
> To help us with our inner sight.
> A purple candle anointed,
> Blue Moon is on the wick.
> The incense is burning steady,

Summer Rain is what we picked.
Our protection now is all in place,
Our minds are open and clear.
Please send to us the wisdom,
And understanding of what we hear.
So Mote It Be.

INCANTATION TWO:

Now in this mojo we place and keep,
The tokens to represent the powers we seek.
We'll bury it soon, deep in the ground,
With hope and thanks for powers to abound.
So Mote It Be.

○ ◐ ● ◑ ○

The Laughing Brew

Coven Ritual (Yellow/Blue)
by Crystal Ball

MAGICKAL INTENTION: To restore harmony, happiness, and healing to the soul.

TIME: Full Moon in August, Sun hour

TOOLS: One yellow candle, Summer Rain oil, Mediterranean Magick incense, one can of frozen pineapple juice, one banana, three cans of 7-Up, a leakproof cauldron, one pound of dry ice, a chalice for each participant, and a ladle.

INSTRUCTIONS: Call a full circle. Anoint the candle with the Summer Rain oil. Light the incense and the candle. Place the ingredients into the cauldron along with the dry ice. The High Priestess should instruct the participants to close their eyes and relax. She asks you to recall a moment in time when you were really happy. Recall a time when you felt physically exceptional. Recall a time when you felt peaceful and balanced. Hold that image in your mind. Visualize the way you looked and felt. Pour the smoking brew into each chalice. Recite the incantation as a group and drink the potion. It will make even the saddest person feel like new again.

INCANTATION:

No longer will I spit or whine,
Take me to the laughing times.
Potion make motion in my spine,
Life be sweet and harmony shine.
Brew be tender,
Brew be kind,
Take me back,
To the laughing times.
So Mote It Be.

The Witch's Closet

Coven Ritual (Gold)
by Sister Moon

MAGICKAL INTENTION: To share spells and wisdom of the Craft.

TIME: Full Moon in August, Sun hour

TOOLS: One gold candle, Mediterranean Magick oil and incense, and one of the following for each participant: small box, assorted pieces of wrapping paper, assorted herbs, assorted magickal stones, and an assortment of things that are found in nature.

INSTRUCTIONS: Anoint the candle with the Mediterranean Magick oil. Light the candle and the incense. Place one herb, one stone and one item of nature in each box. Wrap each box in a piece of wrapping paper. Place the boxes in the center of the circle and recite the incantation. Link hands and circle the boxes.

Each Witch must close her eyes and select a box. Each participant must immediately write a spell that incorporates the color of the paper the box was wrapped in and the box's contents.

Within the hour, each Witch will perform her spell. The Coven must vote on which spell is best. The winner will receive custody of the Coven's Grand Grimoire for one full year.

INCANTATION:

> Within the closet of the Witch,
> Are spiders, scorpions, tools, and pitch.
> Wrap them all in the colors of twelve,
> To inspire the Witch to conjure and delve.
> Round and round the magick will turn,
> Performing spells that spark and burn.
> Channel the power that these inspire,
> Knowledge and witchcraft are required.
> Write the words and cast the spell,
> For all the Witches to foretell.
> Of the power of the Poet's Moon,
> That Witches gather to charm and swoon.
> Praise the Goddess and this night,
> For spinning spells into twilight.
> Merriment of sisters casting this hour,

Creating the magick, uniting in power.
So Mote It Be.

○ ◑ ● ◐ ○

Accept Me

Solitary Ritual (Green/White)
by Aquila Eagle

MAGICKAL INTENTION: To inspire the world to accept religious and personal freedom.

TIME: Full Moon in August, Mercury hour

TOOLS: One white candle, Criss Cross oil, Helping Hand oil, Criss Cross incense, Helping Hand incenses, a pinch each of lemon balm and coconut, one mortar and pestle, an aquamarine, an emerald, an apache's tear, and one red flannel mojo.

INSTRUCTIONS: Anoint the candle with Helping Hand oil. Light the candle and the combination of incenses. Combine three drops of each oil with the herbs in the mortar and pestle and grind it all together. Add the stones. Place all ingredients in the red flannel mojo. Pass the mojo in deosil motion three times through the incense smoke while reciting incantation. Carry the mojo with you and pass it through the incense every Poet's Moon.

INCANTATION:
>Freedom is what I long to find,
>From all people with a closed mind.
>Put inside, wrapped and tied,

My choices will be protected.
Freedom to do what's right for me,
Acceptance will now abound.
Judgment will not turn the key,
But tolerance will draw it down.
So Mote It Be.

○ ◐ ● ◑ ○

Demons in Drag

Solitary Ritual (Black)
by Sister Moon

MAGICKAL INTENTION: To remove negative imagery.

TIME: Hare Moon in August, Saturn hour

TOOLS: One red candle, one black candle, Mandrake oil, JuJu incense, a mirror that is large enough to reflect your entire body, black lipstick, one wand of rolled sage, and a white cloth.

INSTRUCTIONS: Anoint the candles with Mandrake oil. Turn out all the lamps so the candles will be your only light source. Light the candles and the incense. Place the candles on each side of yourself and face the mirror. With the black lipstick, draw the outline of your head and body in the mirror. Lightly color in the image with the lipstick. With the white cloth, wipe the lipstick off of the mirror from the parts of your face and body that you like. Holding the sage wand in your power hand, inscribe a widdershins circle around the image in the mirror and recite the incantation. With every three rotations around the mirror, wipe away more black from your reflection, leaving the original outline. As you do this, the negative image you have of yourself will be removed. Do this until your entire reflection is cleared and then stand inside the outline once again. Burn the white cloth, and repeat the incantation twice.

INCANTATION:

> Demons in drag,
> Hosted by hag.
> Release the shame,
> By fire and flame.
> Black be gone,
> New image be strong.
> Bless my face,
> As I erase.
> Body be right,
> As I invite.
> Beauty of heart,
> Invoked in the dark.
> So Mote It Be.

Little Guardian

Solitary or Coven Ritual (Blue)
by Raiya

MAGICKAL INTENTION: A spell to ask the Faeries to protect your animals.

TIME: Full Moon in August, Mercury hour

TOOLS: One blue candle, Dancing Faeries incense and oil, three-quarters of a teaspoon each of cowslip, primrose, and jasmine, boiling water for a generous cup of tea, a tea strainer, your favorite cup, one small bowl of milk, and one very green emerald or one tiger's eye stone.

INSTRUCTIONS: This spell involves Faery magick. Whenever dealing with Faeries, do not make loud or sudden noises with bells or anything that might frighten them away. Before working with any outside entities, perform a general protection spell for yourself using Astral Projection incense.

To begin, cast a circle. Anoint the candle with the oil. Light the candle and the incense. Combine herbs and place them in the tea strainer. Pour boiling water over the strainer into the cup. Put the bowl of milk and the stone in the North just outside your circle.

Allow your brain to slow down and enter a meditative state. Once you are relaxed and your mind is open, begin drinking your tea. Take five sips and recite the incantation. Do this for a total of five times. (The number five is sacred to the Faeries.) From time to time, leave out a bowl of milk or some fresh butter to show thanks to your "little guardian."

INCANTATION:

Bean-Tighe, Gnomes, and Vasily,
In my hour of need, come to me.
I ask your aid in caring for,
The animal(s) I so adore.
The Gruagach, Zips, and Masseriol,
This Witch summons thee, hear her call.
When I am gone, keep a watchful eye,
Protect my pet from what evil passes by.

I offer this stone as a gift to you,
And to show my thanks, I'll fill the bowl anew.
Please keep my animal out of harm's way,
I ask you guard him [her] night and day.
So Mote It Be.

○ ◐ ● ◑ ○

Third Eye Incense

Solitary or Coven Ritual (Purple)
by Willow

MAGICKAL INTENTION: To create incense that will intensify psychic powers.

TIME: Full Moon in August, Moon hour

TOOLS: One purple candle, frankincense and myrrh resin, a mortar and pestle, a pinch each of peppermint, star anise, lemongrass, mugwort, and flax, red and blue dyes (optional) and rose oil.

INSTRUCTIONS: Light the candle. Grind the resins in the mortar and pestle. As you do this, focus your energy on intense psychic powers. Add the herbs and grind them to a fine powder. Direct all of your psychic energy into this mixture. Add the dyes and a few drops of rose oil, and mix thoroughly. When the incense is completely dry (this may take up to three days), recite the incantation over the mixture three times in your most powerful voice. As you do this, mix the incense with your hands, feeling your psychic energy flow from your body and through the tips of your fingers and into the incense. Store the incense in a tightly capped jar. Burn the incense whenever you desire strong, intense psychic energy.

INCANTATION:

By the power of the Moon,
I charge this incense with intense psychic energy.
Wherever the fire may lick this blend,
All will be known to those who seek
Psychic powers will intensify,
Third eye will open wide.
This is my will, So Mote It Be.

FOURTEEN

The Fire Moon

○ ◐ ● ◑ ○

Raise the Moon in scarlet haze,
Greet the autumn with a blaze.
Release the magick of your desire,
Beneath the orb that rains of fire.

The Full Moon in September is known as The Fire Moon. This is a time to perform rituals dealing with change, bountiful harvests, dancing, gardening, oracles, divining, rededication of Wiccan tools, youth, discovering hidden treasures, thankfulness, cleansing in general, ambitions, rituals of gratitude to the Deities for blessings, and rituals that honor the God. This is also a time to banish negativity on every level, any type of addiction, uselessness, and unwanted relationships.

You're Fired!

Coven Ritual (Gray)
by Sister Moon

MAGICKAL INTENTION: To banish the old, useless things. This spell will not hurt anyone. It will simply banish the negative things or people from your life.

TIME: Full Moon in September, Mars hour

TOOLS: A small bonfire, a gray candle, Banishing oil, Dragon's Fire incense, a square cardboard box with a lid, a small mirror, glue, a black piece of paper with the words "You're Fired," written on it, and ten pieces of gray paper for each member with the words "Pink Slip," written on them, and some strong tape.

INSTRUCTIONS: Light the bonfire. Anoint the candle with the oil. Light the candle and the incense. Glue the mirror to the lid of the box. Place the black paper into the box. On the gray paper, write each thing that you want to be rid of. Be specific and use only one slip for each item. Anoint them with Banishing oil. Recite Incantation One then toss them into the bonfire. Recite Incantation Two. When the bonfire has gone out and is completely cooled, scoop some ashes into the box and seal it shut with tape. Bury the box and recite Incantation One over it.

INCANTATION ONE:
> From the winter's ice to summer's fire,
> I call the Gathering to aid my desire.
> Bind the negative in cornered tomb,
> To receive the bounty of its gloom.
> Mirror its face so it will see,

The effect it used to have on me.
Join in unison with all the foes,
From ashes to ashes, out you go!
So Mote It Be.

INCANTATION TWO:

Out you go, negativity,
And in your place, serenity.
So Mote It Be.

○ ◑ ● ◑ ○

The New Start

Solitary or Coven Ritual (White)
by Indigo

MAGICKAL INTENTION: To rededicate Wiccan tools so they are clean and grounded.

TIME: Full Moon in September, Moon hour

TOOLS: A white piece of cotton material that measures approximately three feet by three feet, four citrines, all of the tools you wish to consecrate, one white candle, Banishing oil, Amulet incense, bowl of consecrated water, and three pinches of sea salt.

INSTRUCTIONS: Go outside to an area where you can leave items undisturbed for twenty-four hours. Place the cloth on the ground with the corners aligned with the four quadrants. Place a stone in each of the corners. Lay out the tools on the cloth. Cast a circle around the area. Anoint the candle with the oil. Light the incense and the candle. Add the salt to the consecrated water. Place three drops of the salt water on each tool and then anoint them with the oil. Leave the tools to dry on the cloth. Recite the incantation three times. Do not blow out the candle; allow it to burn out. Leave everything undisturbed for twenty-four hours.

INCANTATION:

> Angels of the quadrants come,
> Use your powers all as one.
> With the light of moon and sun,
> Forces of evil from them shall run.
> Twenty-four hours they will stay,
> Make them pure as the new day.
> Replenish these tools within the hour,
> Give to them unyielding power.
> So Mote It Be.

Thankfulness

Solitary or Coven Ritual (Gold)
by Astra

MAGICKAL INTENTION: To give thanks to the Goddess and God for the blessings in your life.

TIME: Full Moon in September, Moon hour

TOOLS: One gold candle, Van Van oil, a purple marker, a dozen four-inch squares of gold parchment, a tablespoon each of bayberry, bamboo, and cabbage, and a lighter.

INSTRUCTIONS: Anoint the candle with the Van Van oil. Light the candle. With the purple marker, write on each piece of gold parchment something that you are thankful for. Fold the papers in half and seal each one with the Van Van oil. Dig a hole in the earth about six inches deep and about five inches wide. Place the parchment in the hole, and add the herbs. Recite the incantation and set the parchment on fire. Once everything is reduced to ashes, cover it with earth.

INCANTATION:

> Mother Earth, I give to you what you gave to me.
> I return my blessings thankfully.
> I ask that acknowledgment of the Goddess bring
> my life future blessings.
> See my gratitude rise upon the fiery smoke rings.
> By the power of three by three, I give my thanks.
> I give back to you what you gave to me,
> Thankfully.
> So Mote It Be.

One Clean Sweep

Solitary or Coven Ritual (White)
by Sister Moon

MAGICKAL INTENTION: To cleanse your life.

TIME: Full Moon in September, Mars hour. To be performed outside.

TOOLS: One white candle, Exodus oil, Holy Smoke incense, a ritual broom, holy water, a twenty-inch black cord for each participant and a hole in the earth.

INSTRUCTIONS: Anoint the candle with Exodus oil. Light the candle and the incense. Sweep the ritual area with the broom. Sprinkle the inside of the magick circle with holy water.

Visualize all of the things you would like to purify or eliminate from your life. Tie a knot in a black cord for each thing you would like to remove from your life. Anoint each knot with Exodus oil. Pass the cord through the incense smoke in widdershins motion thirteen times. Recite the incantation.

Set the cord alight using the white candle. Make sure each knot has burned before dropping the remains of cord into the hole. Fill the hole with dirt. Sprinkle the area with holy water, and recite the incantation one final time.

INCANTATION:

> Black and void, I knot away,
> All that I want to clean away.
> I tie this knot and put to rest,
> The soiled energy that was a pest.
> My life now free from this woe,
> Knowing that I have cleansed my soul.
> I ignite the flame to this cord,
> From knot to ash this is my sword.
> Buried within the earth so deep,
> I've cleansed my life with one clean
>   sweep.
> So Mote It Be.

○ ◑ ● ◐ ○

Free at Last!

Solitary or Coven Ritual (Gray)
by Ivy

MAGICKAL INTENTION: To rid yourself of an addiction.

TIME: Hare Moon in September, Saturn hour

TOOLS: One white candle, one gray candle, Exodus oil, Banishing incense, an amethyst, three pinches each of myrrh, nutmeg, and juniper berries, and one red mojo.

INSTRUCTIONS: Cast a full circle. Anoint both candles with Exodus oil. Light the candles and the incense. Anoint the amethyst stone with the oil and visualize yourself being free of any addiction that you are banishing. Put the three herbs and the amethyst into the mojo. Continue visualizing yourself free of the addiction and recite Incantation One three times over the mojo.

Keep the mojo with you at all times. If the addictive desires rise, take out the mojo, hold it close to you, and repeat Incantation Two.

INCANTATION ONE:
> By the powers of three by three,
> Take this habit far from me.
> Take me from the thoughts of need,
> Habits no more will I feed.
> This is my will, So Mote It Be.

INCANTATION TWO:
> I am an ex-[state addiction],
> By the powers of three by three,
> Take these thoughts far from me.
> This is my will, So Mote It Be.

○ ◑ ● ◐ ○

Dig Those Gems

Solitary or Coven Ritual (Purple/Gold)
by Sister Moon

MAGICKAL INTENTION: A magickal talisman to help discover hidden treasures.

TIME: Full Moon in September, Moon hour

TOOLS: Three stones you have found, one gold candle, Witch oil, Isis incense, a small pendulum, and a red flannel mojo.

INSTRUCTIONS: Before the full moon, go into a sacred area and dig for three stones that you find unique or beautiful. They must be given freely from earth to you. If there is any trouble in retrieving them from the ground, leave them be. Clean them and let them be dormant until the Fire Moon.

Anoint the candle with Witch oil. Light the candle and the incense. Place the three stones and the small pendulum in the mojo. Pass the mojo in deosil motion through the incense smoke, and recite the incantation.

Keep the mojo in your pocket. Whenever looking for buried treasures, whether it is in an antiques store or on the ocean floor, the mojo will become hot. At that point, take the pendulum from the mojo and use it to divine your treasure. You will not be disappointed in the riches you will find.

INCANTATION:
> Take me to the land of honey,
> Find me wealth, find me money.

Rocks turn hot within the flannel,
Be my guide, be my channel.
Pendulum swing towards the gold,
Rocks turn hot, rocks turn cold.
Stones of earth be my treasure,
Lead me to worldly pleasures.
So Mote It Be.

○ ◐ ● ◑ ○

The Flame Dance

Solitary or Ritual (Yellow)
by Nova

MAGICKAL INTENTION: To celebrate the drastic changes in one's life and find the strength to accept the change.

TIME: Full Moon in September, Jupiter hour

TOOLS: An open space to build a large bonfire, lots of wood, matches, Easy Life oil, Easy Life incense, a handful of witches grass, and three petals from a columbine.

INSTRUCTIONS: This ritual may be performed skyclad if you wish. Build a bonfire in a space that is open but private. Throw the incense, witch's grass, columbine petals, and three drops of Easy Life oil into the fire.

Dance around the fire while reciting the incantation. Remember, this is a celebration as well as a strength dance. Let all your joy and frustration out. Rejoice in the celebration of change during this Fire moon. Recite the incantation over and over until an overwhelming feeling of tranquility comes over you.

INCANTATION:

>Change may be scary and sometimes sad,
>But we must remember change is not bad.
>Change is a serious matter, not a jest,
>And change is always for the best.
>In the days ahead please help me find,
>The strength I feel has been left behind.
>And give me the courage to enjoy,
>The exciting new beginning I employ.
>I must remember not to shy away,
>At the uncertainty in the coming days.
>So Mote It Be.

FIFTEEN

Mabon

The winsome sound of the howling jackal,
Witch's will spurn, coddle and cackle.
Feel the magick down the spine,
Open the door but don't look behind.

Mabon is on September 21 or 22. It is a minor Sabbat. This is the time to perform rituals dealing with personal balance, emotions and mental health, all areas of earth, all areas of water, honoring deceased family members, binding problems, and banishing negative energy, creating new wands, perfection, destruction of fears and negative emotions, new identities, wishes, reflection and image magick, and employment.

Ties That Bind

Solitary or Coven Ritual (Black)
by Ariel

MAGICKAL INTENTION: To bind negative energies as to put an end to problems.

TIME: September 21 or 22, Jupiter hour

TOOLS: One black candle, Dragon's Fire oil, Obsidian incense, one nine-inch square piece of white parchment, a pen with black ink, one twenty-seven-inch piece of black ribbon, and a lilac bush.

INSTRUCTIONS: Anoint the black candle with the Dragon's Fire oil. Light the candle and the incense. With the black pen, write all of the negative things or problems that are affecting your life on the parchment. Roll the parchment into a scroll and bind it tightly with the black ribbon. Pass the scroll in widdershins motion through the incense smoke thirteen times while reciting the incantation. Bury the parchment beneath the lilac bush. Your problems will be bound until the scroll is decomposed into the earth.

INCANTATION:

> Take these problems, fears and doubts,
> Bind them now inside and out.
> Release me from this negative plight,
> Remove the darkness from this night.
> Leave me positive in my thoughts,
> A balanced life is what I've sought.
> The dark is gone and buried deep,
> Removed forever and put to sleep.
> So Mote It Be.

○ ◐ ● ◑ ○

The Wishing Well

Solitary or Coven Ritual (Purple)
by Sister Moon

MAGICKAL INTENTION: Wishing magick.

TIME: September 21 or 22, Sun hour

TOOLS: One purple candle, Witching oil, Autumn Aspen incense, a wooden bucket or a wishing well, water, and a penny, nickel, dime, and quarter for each participant.

INSTRUCTIONS: Anoint the candle with the oil. Light the candle and the incense. Make sure there is water in the bucket or in the wishing well.

Pick up the penny, make a wish for your spiritual self, recite Incantation One, and toss it into the water. Take up the nickel, make a statement of thankfulness to the Goddess and God, recite Incantation One, and toss it into the water. Take up the dime, make a wish for a child, recite Incantation One, and toss it into the water. Take up the quarter, state what you intend to do to improve your home, neighborhood, or the world in one year's time, recite Incantations One and Two, and toss the quarter into the water.

If a wishing well was used, leave the coins with one final blessing and do not return for one full year. If a wooden bucket was used, dig a hole near a weeping willow, bury the coins and the water, and leave it with one final blessing.

INCANTATION ONE:
> Coin for God, Wish for Spirit,

Coin for Goddess, Mother of All.
Coin for God, Wish for Children,
Coin for Goddess, Prophet for Fall.

INCANTATION TWO:
Copper and silver cast in well,
Wishes and honors conceived in spell.
So Mote It Be.

○ ◑ ● ◐ ○

Water

Coven Ritual (Gray/ Black)
by Luna

MAGICKAL INTENTION: To use the magick of water to put an end to problems and wash away all negative energy.

TIME: September 21 or 22, Saturn hour

TOOLS: A black candle, Widdershins oil, Drive and Bind incense, one tablespoon each of adder's tongue, barley, chives, dandelion, ephedra, fennel, ginseng, hazel, and lady's slipper, a bag of charcoal, large freshly fallen leaves (they must not be dry), and a ball of twine or yarn.

INSTRUCTIONS: Anoint the candle with Widdershins oil. Light the candle and incense. Combine the nine herbs and set aside.

Each participant takes a piece of charcoal and imagines it as a certain problem or negative aspect in her or his life. (Use as many pieces of charcoal as needed.) Place each charcoal on a leaf and sprinkle the herb mixture on top of it. The herbs will cancel out all negativity.

Wrap the leaves around the pieces of charcoal and use the twine to tie them into little packages.

Take the little bundles to a flowing body of water, preferably a river. Say the incantation and then release the bundles into the water.

INCANTATION:

We take our negative thoughts and signify them as
  black lumps of coal.
Dark and harmful we do not need their pull.
To take the dark flair we pour on our potion of light,
The power of three by three will aid us in our fight.
We tie the earth's skin to indicate the season,
We use the water element for powerful reason.
Release the bundles of negativity to be covered in
  cleansing water,
Negativity is banished and love is replaced.
So Mote It Be.

○ ◑ ● ◐ ○

Phantoms of Fear

Solitary or Coven Ritual (Black)
by Crystal Ball

MAGICKAL INTENTION: A ritual to destroy fear and negative emotions.

TIME: September 21 or 22, Saturn hour

TOOLS: One black candle, Black Musk oil, Obsidian incense, a picture of a badger, a hematite, a pinch of belladonna, a pinch of birch, and a very small red flannel mojo.

INSTRUCTIONS: Anoint the candle with Black Musk oil. Light the candle and the incense. Place the picture, hematite, belladonna, and birch into the red mojo. Visualize all negative emotions and fears being destroyed. Pass the mojo in deosil motion through the incense smoke while reciting the incantation. Wear the mojo over your heart whenever you feel negative or fearful.

INCANTATION:

> Phantoms that creep into my fear,
> Now will vanish and disappear.
> I wear the potion over my heart,
> Where negativity will never start.
> Mabon sabbat destroys the foul,
> Of fear and evil that lurks and prowls.
> No longer living near my thought,
> Phantoms be gone, I destroy the lot.
> So Mote It Be.

Witch's Honor

Coven Ritual (Purple)
by Sister Moon

MAGICKAL INTENTION: To receive wisdom from Witches of the past.

TIME: September 21 or 22, Mercury hour

TOOLS: Thirteen purple candles, Midnight oil, a large cauldron, thirteen ladles of graveyard dirt (real dirt from a graveyard, not the herb), thirteen pinches of rosemary, thirteen pinches of sea salt, thirteen pieces of devil's shoestring, thirteen black hairs from a Witch's familiar (remember, use only hair that has been combed out or has fallen out naturally), and thirteen pieces of purple paper, each inscribed with the names of a Witch who has crossed over. If you do not know the names of thirteen Witches that have crossed, use these: Sybil, Hectate, Fate, Sarah, Windborne, Jinx, Opal, Mary of Salem, Cat of Nine Tales, Dolly, Spirit, Azure, and Disciple.

INSTRUCTIONS: Anoint the thirteen candles with Midnight oil. Light the candles and place them in a large circle around the cauldron. Place the dirt in the cauldron and add the rosemary, salt, devil's shoestring, hairs, and incense. Light the incense.

As the cauldron is smoking, all participants hold hands and form a circle. Recite the name on each piece of paper and cast them into the cauldron. Recite the incantation.

Visualize the Witches of Honor coming to you now. See them rise from the ashes. Ask that their powers and wisdom be given to you. You will sense, see, or hear what your wisdom is to be. Thank the Witches for their valuable words and then bury the contents of the cauldron inside the circle after the ashes have cooled.

INCANTATION:

> We call upon the Witches of old,
> Let your wisdom now be told.
> Thirteen names cast into the fire,
> Bring to us what we desire.
> Reveal the wisdom so we may learn,
> Speak to us as the offering burns.

Mabon sabbat in all its power,
Come to us this Mercury hour.
We honor your presence upon this night,
With thirteen candles of fiery light.
Walk with us upon the earth,
Bestow your wisdom and your mirth.
So Mote It Be.

○ ◐ ● ◑ ○

Sticks and Stones

Solitary or Coven Ritual (Purple)
by Raven

MAGICKAL INTENTION: To create a magickal wand.

TIME: September 21 or 22, Moon hour

TOOLS: One purple candle, Dragon's Fire oil, Witch incense, a perfectly straight piece of wood approximately seven to twelve inches in length that has been stained with wood stain, seven small magickal stones that have already been charged in the moonlight, a hot glue gun and glue sticks, eighteen strips of bendable wire, and two quartz crystals.

INSTRUCTIONS: Anointing the candle with Dragon's Fire oil. Light the candle and the incense. Feel free to create your wand in the way it is pleasing to you. Using the hot glue gun and glue sticks, attach the stones to the wood. Wrap the wire around the stones while the glue is still warm. Attach the quartz crystals to each end of the wand. Pass the wand in deosil motion thirteen times through the incense smoke while reciting the incantation.

After the wand is completely finished, place it in a dark place until the next Full Moon. Charge the wand in the moonlight and use as desired.

INCANTATION:

> Seven stones and earthly wood,
> Channel the magick as it should.
> Harness the power within this wand,
> Adhere to me and be my bond.
> Unleash the magick as I invoke,
> Concentrated energy with every stroke.
> Charged by earth and Mabon power,
> May Deities bless by day and hour.
> Wand of earth, wand of stone,
> Harvest the magick I have grown.
> Incense of Witch and Dragon's Fire,
> Release the magick of my desire.
> So Mote It Be.

○ ◐ ● ◑ ○

Problems Away

Solitary or Coven Ritual (Gold/White)
by Journey

MAGICKAL INTENTION: To dispel problems.

TIME: September 21 or 22, Mars Hour

TOOLS: One gold candle, Amulet oil, one diced garlic clove, one diced onion, one diced hot chile pepper, one piece of gingerroot, thirteen black peppercorns, one tablespoon of salt, one cup of white vinegar, a cast-iron cauldron, Success incense, a wooden spoon, a strainer, and a bottle with a lid or cork.

INSTRUCTIONS: Anoint the candle with Amulet oil. Place the garlic, onion, chile pepper, ginger, peppercorns, salt, and vinegar in the cauldron.

Heat the cauldron over a low fire. Light the candle and the incense. Keep incense lit the entire time potion is brewing.

Stir the potion in widdershins motion with the wooden spoon, and repeat the incantation three times.

When the potion is done, strain it into the bottle and let it sit undisturbed for seven days. On the eighth day, use it to anoint the outside corners of your home, place of business, car, garden, and so on—any area where you feel there are problems. Repeat the incantation as you anoint.

INCANTATION:

> Problems, problems I abhor,
> This potent spell will show them the door.
> Fumes so acrid they cannot stay,
> Successfully turn the problems away.
> Dispel them! Dispel them!
> Do as I say.
> Problems, problems be no more!
> Problems, problems be no more!
> Problems, problems be no more!
> So Mote It Be!

SIXTEEN

The Harvest Moon

Plentiful Earth is now at rest,
Death and dormant reflects due west.
Witches walk the graves and the tombs,
And the ghosts will rise to Harvest the Moon.

The Full Moon in October is known as The Harvest Moon. This is a time to perform rituals dealing with protection during times of travel, the sixth chakra, honoring the deceased, clocks, brooms, calendars, graveyards, employment, honoring all winged creatures, healing and good health, clearings, nesting, potions and brews, communication with the deceased, and homage to the God. This is also a time to banish grieving, suffering, negativity in any form, fears, and phobias.

Wings of Safety

Solitary or Coven Ritual (Blue)
by Lyra

MAGICKAL INTENTION: For protection during times of travel.

TIME: Full Moon in October, Mercury hour.

TOOLS: One large blue candle, Protection From Thieves oil, Dove's Flight incense, a galangal root, needles from a Norfolk pine tree, a few juniper berries, and a red flannel mojo.

INSTRUCTIONS: Anoint the candle with the oil. Light the candle and the incense. Place the root, pine needles, and berries in the red flannel mojo. Repeat the incantation three times while passing the mojo in deosil motion through the incense smoke. Carry the mojo with you anytime you travel. Pass the mojo through incense smoke every full moon to keep it energized.

INCANTATION:

> In this bag filled with charms,
> To all that go, will bring no harm.
> Keep me safe and in Your care,
> Lord and Lady, hear my prayer.
> So Mote It Be.

○ ◐ ● ◑ ○

Blood on the Moon

Coven Ritual (Purple/Blue)
by Sister Moon

MAGICKAL INTENTION: A ritual to honor the deceased.

TIME: Full Moon in October, Moon hour

TOOLS: Ten purple candles, Witch oil, a large cauldron, a picture of the deceased to be honored, Wicca incense, white parchment, a pen with black ink, and a pinch each of anise, and lavender, and apple, and pumpkin seeds.

INSTRUCTIONS: Anoint the candles with Witch oil. Place the candles in a circle around the cauldron. Place each picture of a deceased loved one near a candle. Light the candles; place the incense in the cauldron and light it. Recite Incantation One and invite the spirits of the deceased into the circle. When you feel their presence, cast the anise, lavender, and apple and pumpkin seeds into the cauldron. All participants link hands and recite Incantation Two. Circle around the cauldron once and raise hands into the air to release the spirits.

INCANTATION ONE:

> The circle around the pearly moon,
> Pulls the spirits from their tombs.
> We invite you to our circle of love,
> This Harvest Moon—The Circle of Blood.
> We honor you and hold you near,
> Join us now, the veil is sheer.
> Open your heart and receive us well,
> Blood on the Moon, we cast this spell.
> So Mote It Be.

INCANTATION TWO:

> Welcome loved ones, friends and guests,
> Touch our hearts as you do best.
> Blessings and prayers we offer to you,
> And thank you for these minutes so few.
> So Mote It Be.

○ ◐ ● ◑ ○

The Witch's Nest

Coven Ritual (Brown/Orange)
by Daughter of Dragons

MAGICKAL INTENTION: Ritual of honor for the birds of nature.

TIME: Full Moon in October, Mercury hour

TOOLS: One brown candle, Nefertite oil, Magnet incense, some small branches and twigs, hair from your hairbrush, mud, fallen leaves, a four-by-six-inch piece of wood, and glue.

INSTRUCTIONS: Anoint the brown candle with the oil. Light the candle and the incense. Use the twigs and branches to create a birds' nest; use the hair, mud and leaves to give the nest substance.

Next, glue the two small bowls to the piece of wood; these will hold birdseed and water. Then glue the nest to the wood. Pass the whole thing in deosil motion three times through the incense smoke and recite the incantation.

After your birds' nest is complete, fill the bowls with birdseed and water. Place the nest in a tree where it will be sheltered from the elements.

INCANTATION:

> For all our friends with feathers and wings,
> We welcome you to nest and sing.
> We bless this home with water and seed,
> And welcome you to shelter and feed.
> We ask the Goddess to create and bless,
> A place of refuge and maternal nest.
> The hands that built your humble home,
> Are Witches that contribute from their comb.
> Protect this house by wind and fire,
> Earth and water and angels' choir.
> Keep all creatures big and small,
> Safe from winter's bitter claw.
> Birds of feather safely fly,
> To this home and to the sky.
> From the hands of Witches' weave,
> A sacred space that cannot thieve.
> Protection for all that Goddess will bless,
> And the feathered friends within this nest.
> So Mote It Be.

The Job Squad

Coven Ritual (Green)
by Crystal Ball

MAGICKAL INTENTION: To gain employment.

TIME: Full Moon in October, Jupiter hour

TOOLS: Four green candles, Forest Nymph oil, Woodlands incense, a large cauldron, a pinch each of basil, mandrake, celery, and poppy, and four pinches of saltpeter.

INSTRUCTIONS: Anoint each of the candles with Forest Nymph oil. Light the candles. Place the incense into the cauldron and light it.

One participant should stand in each of the four directions. The person in need of employment should stand closest to the cauldron. The person in the north recites Incantation One and casts the basil into the cauldron. The person in the south recites Incantation Two and casts the mandrake into the cauldron. The person in the east recites Incantation Three and casts the celery into the cauldron. The person in the west recites Incantation Four and casts the poppy into the cauldron. The person in need of employment recites Incantation Five. One by one, the participants cast saltpeter into the cauldron, creating a puff of smoke. All recite Incantation Six. The person in need of employment finishes by reciting Incantation Seven.

INCANTATION ONE:
> Northern Tower—I invoke thee,
> May the richness of earth envelop me.
> So Mote It Be.

INCANTATION TWO:
> Southern Tower—I invoke thee,
> May the fires of the Sun radiate from me.
> So Mote It Be.

INCANTATION THREE:
> Eastern Tower—I invoke thee,
> May the winds of prosperity carry me.
> So Mote It Be.

INCANTATION FOUR:
>Western Tower—I invoke thee,
>May the waters of good fortune rain upon me.
>So Mote It Be.

INCANTATION FIVE:
>All the towers—gathered four,
>Grant me the employment that I adore.
>So Mote It Be.

INCANTATION SIX:
>Witches within the mighty towers,
>Release your magick this Jupiter hour.
>So Mote It Be.

INCANTATION SEVEN:
>I thank thee towers—gathered four,
>I carry your magick as I explore.
>So Mote It Be.

○ ◑ ● ◑ ○

Negative Knots

Coven Ritual (Gray)
by Luna

MAGICKAL INTENTION: To banish negative energy from your life and to bring forth a harvest of strong, positive energy.

TIME: Hare Moon in October, Moon hour

TOOLS: One large gray candle, Banishing oil, three tablespoons (or more) of Drive Away Evil incense, a two-foot-long strip of cloth or thin rope for each participant, and a cauldron.

INSTRUCTIONS: Anoint the candle with Banishing oil. Light the candle and the incense. Each member should tie three knots in his or her piece of the cloth or rope while visualizing the negative energies that he or she would like to eliminate. Then tie the two ends of the cloth together to make a circle.

Pass each cloth three times in widdershins motion through the incense smoke, and recite the incantation. Light the entire cloth or rope on fire and place it in the cauldron to burn. While it is burning, visualize all of the negative energies vanishing from your life. Be sure to stand away from the smoke, because negative energy stinks!

INCANTATION:

> The knots of three release from me,
> And send good positive energy.
> With each tightening of the cloth,
> The anger and fighting stops.
> Three by three the knots are tied,
> As the Witches gladly abide.
> The power surges and becomes complete,
> The circle of negativity feels the heat.
> The last knot tied links a circle formed,
> The cloth burns flames of evil scorned.
> Watches the evil go up in smoke,
> A Witch's dream we now evoke.
> So Mote It Be.

Happiness

Solitary or Coven Ritual (Yellow)
by Raiya

MAGICKAL INTENTION: To eliminate depression and increase happiness.

TIME: Full Moon in October, Sun hour

TOOLS: One large yellow candle, Happiness oil, Criss-Cross incense, a pinch each of lavendar and catnip, a mortar and pestle, a tea steeper, a cup of hot water, and a pinch each of chamomile, raspberry, and peppermint.

INSTRUCTIONS: Anoint the candle with Happiness oil. Light the candle and the incense. Place the lavender and catnip in the mortar and grind them to a fine powder. Set the herbs alight, recite the incantation, and let them burn to ash. Combine the chamomile, raspberry, and peppermint in a tea steeper. Place the steeper in the hot water. Drink the tea while visualizing three things that make you happy.

INCANTATION:

> From this being, sadness be gone,
> She has been depressed far too long.
> Happiness fills her, self esteem overtake,
> Looking forward to each day that she wakes.
> Open her eyes and help her see,
> How fun and joyous life can be.
> A positive attitude will be the notion,
> With happiness and joy in this potion.

Lavender and catnip turned to ash,
Ensuring happiness will ever last.
Chamomile, peppermint, and raspberry tea,
Prevents sadness and makes it flee.
This is my will, So Mote It Be.

○ ◑ ● ◐ ○

Health's A-bloomin'

Solitary or Coven Ritual (Yellow/Orange)
by Ariel

MAGICKAL INTENTION: To improve your health.

TIME: Hare Moon in October, Sun hour

TOOLS: One yellow candle, one orange candle, Drawing oil, Radiant Health incense, three pinches each of lime peel, nettles, and a walnut, a small bowl, one turquoise, and a geranium.

INSTRUCTIONS: Anoint the candles with Drawing oil. Light the candles and the incense. Place the lime peel, nettles, and walnut in the bowl and pass it deosil through the incense smoke three times. Next, take the turquoise and pass it in deosil motion through the incense smoke three times. Do the same with the geranium.

Bury the walnut and the turquoise in the geranium's soil, reciting the incantation for each item. Sprinkle the nettles and lime peel on top of the soil, repeating the incantation a third time. Take care of your plant and nurture it; it will then take care of you.

INCANTATION:

> The life I give this plant,
> Let it return to me.
> Let us both grow strong and true,
> Far from disease we both shall be.
> As this plant renews itself,
> So will my health improve.
> So Mote It Be.

SEVENTEEN
Samhain

One day and night the dead shall walk,
And at your door they shall knock.
Invite them in and feed them well,
Share your secrets, for they won't tell.

Samhain is on October 31 and is a major Sabbat. It is also known as All Hallow's Eve. This is the time to perform rituals dealing with communication with the dead, honoring the deceased, rest, contemplation, priorities, banishing evil, releasing earthbound entities, karmic connections, good luck, psychic abilities, divining, the circle of life, art, music, entertainment, priorities, and to pay special homage to the God. Because the real magick begins at midnight on October 31, the magick carries over for a full twenty-four hours to November 1.

The Wake at Widow's Hill

Coven Ritual (Green)
by Tatituba

MAGICKAL INTENTION: For good luck.

TIME: October 31, Midnight hour

TOOLS: Three green candles, All Hallows' oil, All Hallows' incense, a chalice, and three red roses.

INSTRUCTIONS: Go to a graveyard that is on top of a hill (the older the graveyard the better). Find a dual burial site—that of a man who is already buried and that bears his still-living wife's name. If you find a tombstone near a bench or other place to sit, imagine the tears of the widows that have cried there. Anoint the candles with the oil and place them around the wife's side of the tombstone. Light the candles and the incense. Place the chalice in the center of the ring of candles. Place the roses beside the grave. Recite the incantation.

When you feel the presence of an entity, take the candles but leave the chalice and the roses. Return the next day to see if anything has been placed inside the chalice. This chalice is now your good-luck token. Preserve it and keep it with you. Leave the roses as an offering.

INCANTATION:

> The widow's tears for death and sorrow,
> Conjuring power in wake of tomorrow.
> Gather the grief and turn it well,
> To good fortune in widow's spell.

For the dead are roses of three,
To comfort the soul and memory.
But in the center is the chalice,
To fulfill the dreams of a palace.
Fortune and luck fills the cup,
With a mortal gift of good luck.
Cherished always in the Witch's till,
When waking magick on Widow's Hill.
So Mote It Be.

○ ◑ ● ◐ ○

Feast of the Dead

Coven Ritual (Gold/Purple)
by Sister Moon

MAGICKAL INTENTION: Ritual feast for honoring the deceased.

TIME: October 31, Moon hour

TOOLS: One gold candle, one purple candle, All Hallows' oil, All Hallows' incense, twelve plates of your favorite autumn foods, and apple cider. As a centerpiece, use a small wooden coffin with the lid open. Set around the coffin different herbs, spices, and salt and pepper with which to season the food.

INSTRUCTIONS: Anoint both candles with the All Hallows oil. Light the candles and the incense. Place the candles on the east and west sides of the coffin centerpiece. Have the participants sit at the table, the High Priestess at the head. Leave an empty chair and place setting for the dead at the table's foot. Prepare a heaping plate for the empty setting. Link hands and all recite Incantation One before beginnning the feast.

At the end of the feast, all recite Incantation Two. Place all of the remaining herbs and spices into the coffin and close the lid. This will preserve good fortune for the deceased and the participants of the ritual for one full year.

Bury the coffin outside and recite Incantation Two once again. Place the plate for the deceased outside for the animals to feast upon.

INCANTATION ONE:

To the Goddess and God, all of the angels and good spirits, we gather together to celebrate the precious moments of life and the eternal cycle of death to life. We are thankful for the year of bounty we have received, and wish to invite a special ghost with positive energy to feast with us tonight. This is our will. So Mote It Be.

INCANTATION TWO:

Ashes to ashes, dust to dust,
Seed to flower, herb to crust.
Re-open the veil between heaven
and earth,
Farewell to friend, till next you birth.
So Mote It Be.

○ ◑ ● ◐ ○

The Webs of Time

Solitary Ritual (Gold)
by Colleechee

MAGICKAL INTENTION: To understand your karmic connection to a certain person.

TIME: October 31, Mercury hour

TOOLS: Two gold candles, All Hallows' oil, Memory and Hypnotic incenses, an abandoned spiderweb, a 1964 silver dollar, a broken watch or other timepiece, and a red flannel mojo.

INSTRUCTIONS: Anoint the candles with the oil. Light the candles and the incenses. Place the spiderweb, coin, and timepiece into the red flannel mojo. Pass the mojo in deosil motion through the incense smoke while reciting the incantation.

Place the mojo beneath your pillow before going to sleep. Ask the Guides to reveal in your dreams the karmic connection you have with a specific person. Bury the mojo beneath a weeping willow tree within seven days after having the dream.

INCANTATION:

> Time has stopped,
> In the web.
> Tides will flow,
> Tides will ebb.
> Remember when,
> We once knew.
> From long ago,
> Our lives were new.

Take me to,
The time and place.
Of when I first,
Saw your face.
Show to me,
The facts and finds,
Of a different place,
And a different time.
Reveal the past,
Within a dream.
Of the karma,
That I gleam.
So Mote It Be.

Creative Pleasure

Coven Ritual (Orange and Black)
by Luna

MAGICKAL INTENTION: To communicate with the dead through artistic expression.

TIME: October 31, Mercury hour

TOOLS: A small orange candle for each participant, All Hallows' oil, Leopard incense, Attraction incense, a piece of black paper for each participant, a white crayon for each participant, and a container of salt.

INSTRUCTIONS: Anoint the candles with the All Hallows' oil. Light the candles and the incense. All participants sit on the floor in a circle with their piece of paper in front of them. Each participant's crayon should go on one side of her paper, and each candle should be placed opposite each participant. No other lights should be on in the room.

The High Priestess makes a circle of salt around all the participants. Place the incense in the center of the circle. The Coven joins hands and recites the incantation three times. Concentrate and invoke the powers. After the incantation is completed, each person should try to communicate with the spirit world by channeling through the paper. Write or draw whatever comes to mind. After everyone is done, compare the experiences and thank the spirits who came to share with you.

INCANTATION:

> The veil between the worlds is now at its weakest,
> The spirits of the other world are now able to
>   pass into this one.
> The holy salt protects our Coven, keeping us safe
>   until it's done.
> As we watch the dancing flames, we ask the spir-
>   its to join our circle.
> Come share with us your creative pleasure.
> We ask to draw and to record the mystical world
>   that is your treasure.
> Share with us. Show us.
> So Mote It Be.

○ ◐ ● ◑ ○

First Things First

Solitary Ritual (Purple)
by Daughter of Dragons

MAGICKAL INTENTION: To realize your priorities and to keep them in proper order.

TIME: October 31, Venus hour

TOOLS: One purple candle, High John the Conqueror oil, Magick incense, purple parchment, a pen with black ink, and the eye of a peacock feather.

INSTRUCTIONS: Anoint the candle with High John the Conqueror oil. Light the candle and the incense. On the parchment, write, in order, all of the priorities in your life. Make sure they are numbered and they are in the order you desire them. Wrap the eye of the peacock feather in the parchment and pass it through the incense smoke. Recite the incantation. Bury the packet on a high hill by the light of the moon.

INCANTATION:

> First things first,
> For better, for worse.
> I conjure the eye,
> To watch and spy.
> My priorities aligned,
> Like a solid bind.
> I will always cast,
> The beginning to last.
> In the way I live,
> In the way I give.

Keep me aware,
Of the spell I bear.
Never to stray,
From this day.
Upon this hill,
A spell is filled.
First things first,
This spell immersed.
I keep things straight,
My choice, my fate.
So Mote It Be.

○ ◐ ● ◑ ○

Old Haunts

Solitary or Coven Ritual (Gray/Brown)
by Raven

MAGICKAL INTENTION: To release an earthbound entity.

TIME: October 31 or November 1, Mars hour

TOOLS: A cauldron with a small mirror placed in the bottom, Exorcism incense, one gray candle, one white candle, one black candle, Exorcism oil, a tiger's eye, and a hematite.

INSTRUCTIONS: Place the cauldron in the center of the circle. Place a circle of incense around the mirror and light it. Anoint the candles with the exorcism oil. Light the candles. Place one stone in each hand and recite the incantation. Invite the entity you want to release to join the circle. Visualize the spirit coming in and direct the spirit toward the smoldering cauldron. When you feel the entity go into the cauldron, recite the incantation again. Take the ashes of the incense and the mirror out of the cauldron and away from the haunted area immediately. Bury them near a cemetery or other hallowed ground.

INCANTATION:

> Wandering soul, nameless spirit.
> Come to my voice when you hear it.
> Welcome to my circle round,
> Unleash the bonds of where you're bound.
> Enter in this dance of smoke,
> Down and in as I invoke.
> The smoking cauldron is your gate,
> To release your daunted fate.
> The tiger's stone and hematite,
> Protects the Witches in your sight.
> Gather here for your release,
> Spirit gone and haunt to cease.
> So Mote It Be.

The Chosen One

Solitary or Coven Ritual (Purple)
by Sister Moon

MAGICKAL INTENTION: To receive messages from beyond the grave.

TIME: October 31 or November 1, Midnight hour

TOOLS: One small purple candle, White Solstice oil, and Blue Gypsy incense.

INSTRUCTIONS: Go to a graveyard at midnight. Anoint the candle with White Solstice oil. Light the candle and the incense. Place the candle on the tombstone that calls to you. Recite the incantation. Lie upon the grave just as the deceased is laid in the ground and fold your arms over your chest. When you feel a presence, call out, "I am the chosen one." Listen to your message. When the flame of the candle goes out, return to your home. Remember, you will be having some visitors (ghosts) for the night, so don't panic.

INCANTATION:

> When two or more shall gather on All Hallows' Eve,
> A deed must be done for those who believe.
> The dead have been silent for one whole year,
> Now they must speak, and the chosen one shall hear.
> Within the midnight hour you must walk with the
>   dead,
> Their graves of stone will mark their beds.
> Carry a beacon to show you have come,
> Call to them, "I am the chosen one."
> Listen carefully for what you shall hear,
> For it tells your future for one full year.
> Light one candle and leave it on a stone,
> When the flame goes out, return to your home.
> After the dead have spoken on All Hallows Eve,
> They all shall visit your bed and your dreams.
> So Mote It Be.

EIGHTEEN

The Hunter's Moon

Crisp fallen leaves blanket the ground,
Stags and horns are worn as crowns.
Gather the Witches for magick and feast,
To protect our earth and the beasts.

The Full Moon in November is known as The Hunter's Moon. This is a time to perform rituals dealing with the seventh or crown chakra, angels, peace, comfort, kitchens and hearths, sunsets, solving mysteries, siblings, friends, resolving differences, cleansing, purification, wisdom, new employment or profession, protection and replenishment of the natural resources, stones and minerals, animals, weavings, art, altars, and music. This is also a time to banish guilt, laziness, and bad judgment.

Family Ties

Solitary Ritual (Brown)
by Ivy

MAGICKAL INTENTION: To keep family members together and resolve differences.

TIME: Full Moon in November, Moon Hour

TOOLS: One large brown candle, Ravenwood oil, Bending oil, Hearthside incense, a twelve-inch square piece of brown cotton material, one small personal item from each family member, an Apache's tears, three pinches of meadowsweet, and a piece of string one yard in length.

INSTRUCTIONS: Anoint the candle with both oils. Light the candle and the incense. Lay out the piece of brown material and place the personal items in the center of the fabric. Add the Apache's tear and sprinkle with meadowsweet. Recite Incantation One. Roll herbs and stone in the brown material in a cylinder. Bind the contents inside with the string so that nothing will fall out. Anoint the cylinder with Bending oil and pass it in deosil motion through the incense smoke three times. Recite Incantation Two. Bury the cylinder in the front yard of your home, near the front door. This will keep harmony in your home.

INCANTATION ONE:
>Family members near and far,
>Close to heart is where you are.
>Let us not be bitter or sore,
>Open our hearts so the love will pour.
>Anger and strife all be gone,

And send us love to last all year long.
This is my will, So Mote It Be.

INCANTATION TWO:

With these people in my life,
I bind us with love, warm and tight.
Gone are feelings sad and mad,
In this potion to make us glad.
Keep this family all as one,
From now until the days are done.
This is my will, So Mote It Be.

○ ◗ ● ◖ ○

The House That Guilt Built

Coven Ritual (Black)
by Rising Star

MAGICKAL INTENTION: To rid yourself of guilt and the barriers it places upon you.

TIME: Full Moon in November, Saturn hour

TOOLS: One black candle, Banishing oil, Drive and Bind incense, Popsicle sticks, a glue gun and glue, a can of black pepper, and a hand shovel.

INSTRUCTIONS: Perform this ritual outdoors. Anoint the candle with the Banishing oil. Light the candle and the incense. Using the Popsicle sticks and the glue guns, construct a small model house. Write the word *guilt* on each piece of the house. Recall specifically what guilt you carry. Visualize that guilt leaving your hand and going into the Popsicle sticks. As you glue each piece together, allow your guilt to stick to the house.

Sprinkle the house with black pepper. Dig a small hole and place the house in it. Anoint the house with Banishing oil, and set the house on fire. Allow the house to burn to ash as you recite the incantation over and over. Bury the ashes in the hole.

INCANTATION:

> Black as pepper,
> Guilted leper.
> Release and burn,
> This guilt I spurn.
> So Mote It Be.

○ ◑ ● ◐ ○

The Dream Pillow

Solitary or Coven Ritual (Gold)
by Sister Moon

MAGICKAL INTENTION: To inspire wisdom.

TIME: Full Moon in November, Moon hour

TOOLS: One gold candle, Midas oil, Van Van incense, four pieces of cloth that are attractive and are cut into pieces that are approximately three inches by six inches, a needle and white thread, finely ground eyebright, almond, allspice, vanilla, frankincense, myrrh and basil, an earthen bowl, and a piece of white parchment.

INSTRUCTIONS: Anoint the candle with the oil. Light the candle and the incense. Take two pieces of the material and place them so the right sides are together; sew them on three sides to create a sack. Do the same with the other two pieces of material.

Place the herbs in the earthen bowl. Anoint the herbs with Midas oil. Write on the white parchment, asking for wisdom to be bestowed upon you. Set the parchment alight with the candle flame. Place the cooled ashes in the bowl. Recite the incantation over the bowl.

Place the herbs and ashes into the first sack, pass it through the incense smoke, and sew it shut. Place the first bag into the second sack and sew it shut. Recite the incantation once again over the pillow while passing it through the incense smoke. Place the dream pillow over your eyes before sleeping to receive wisdom.

INCANTATION:

> Angels and spirits, I search for truth,
> I ask for wisdom of the sleuth.
> Within the magick of seven herbs,
> I conjure knowledge of the superb.
> An herb to open the mental gates,
> One for compassion in this fate.
> One for psychic powers of blue,
> One to open the soul so true.
> One for dreams of days to come,
> One for freedom to dance and run.
> One for my sisters within this rite,
> To join in perception and our fight.
> I close my eyes to absorb the gift,
> Dreams unfold to wisdom adrift.
> Within the magick and these seams,
> I conjure the knowledge and right to dream.
> So Mote It Be.

○ ◑ ● ◐ ○

Hunting for Peace

Solitary Ritual (Yellow)
by Nova

MAGICKAL INTENTION: To bring peace between constantly argu-
ing siblings.

TIME: Full Moon in November, Moon hour

TOOLS: One large yellow candle for each sibling involved, Eucalyptus oil, Happiness oil, and Easy Life incense.

INSTRUCTIONS: Anoint the candles generously with each of the
oils. Light the incense. Recite the incantation over the candles
while lighting them.

　Give each sibling a candle and have them light it each night before going to bed for seven consecutive days. After the week is over,
they should light the candles whenever they feel frustrated or
angry at each other.

INCANTATION:
　　In the dark of the night,
　　Yellow's joyous light.
　　Shines to bring peace,
　　And put blood's bond at ease.
　　Let the love within shine out,
　　And argument end without a shout.
　　Peace within each heart and mind,
　　That shines the candle forward in time.
　　So Mote It Be.

○ ◐ ● ◑ ○

The Replenishment

Solitary or Coven Ritual (Green)
by Sister Moon

MAGICKAL INTENTION: To replenish the earth and yourself.

TIME: Hare Moon in November, Sun hour

TOOLS: One large green candle, Fertility oil, Woodlands incense, a cauldron, a handful of dried leaves, a handful of dried marigolds, and several pieces of green paper cut into strips.

INSTRUCTIONS: Anoint the candle with Fertility oil. Place the incense inside the cauldron. Light the candle. Place the handful of dried leaves and dried marigolds into the cauldron. Ignite the incense and the leaves. Scatter the green strips of paper in the fire. Recite the incantation. After all has burned to ash, face east and scatter the potion to the wind, reciting the incantation one more time.

INCANTATION:

> Lifeless fruit of flower and trees,
> Return to earth by fire and breeze.
> Time to search for peace and rest,
> Nestled in November's breast.
> Replenish the earth beneath the still,
> Fertile soil will nourish and till.
> Stir the source of life and health,
> Restore the life within myself.
> So Mote It Be.

○ ◐ ● ◑ ○

Signs

Solitary or Coven Ritual (White)
by Phoenix

MAGICKAL INTENTION: To solve a mystery.

TIME: Full Moon in November, Mercury hour

TOOLS: One white candle, Moonlight oil, Mystic Veil incense, and a pair of divining rods.

INSTRUCTIONS: Go to a quiet place in nature. Anoint the candle with the oil. Light the candle and the incense. Concentrate on a specific question that you would like answered. Ask the Guides to reveal each answer to each question that you ask. Recite the incantation. Use the divining rods to determine the direction in which you should start this journey. As you walk along, ask your question out loud. Listen, watch, and sense what your signs are saying. For example, if you have a lost cat, use your divining rods to see which path holds your answer. If you see a leaf blowing to the west, then that is your answer.

Carefully log or remember the answers to each of your questions. When your path becomes silent, consult the divining rods again to see which direction you need to go to continue finding your answers. Continue this journey until all of your questions have been answered. If you do not understand the answer, write it down and consult others in your Coven to help decipher what you received.

INCANTATION:

> I ask the angels to be my guide,
> Solve the mystery that's locked inside.

Be my eyes and be my ears,
Be my senses as I peer.
With each question, show the way,
Turn my night into day.
With each clue, I shall find,
All the answers with your signs.
So Mote It Be.

○ ◐ ● ◑ ○

Protective Wings

Solitary or Coven Ritual (Blue)
by Poseidon

MAGICKAL INTENTION: To have the Angels guard and protect someone.

TIME: Full Moon in November, Sun hour

TOOLS: One blue candle, Protection oil, Angel incense, a picture of the person who needs to be protected, a corn husk, and a naturally fallen white feather.

INSTRUCTIONS: Anoint the candle with the Protection oil. Light the candle and the incense. Place the picture of the person inside the corn husk. Place the white feather on top of the picture. Pass the husk in deosil motion through the incense smoke while reciting the incantation.

Take the corn husk to a body of water and recite the incantation one more time. Place the husk on top of the water and allow it to float away. When you find another white feather upon your path, you will know the Angels are still protecting you.

INCANTATION:

> Husk of corn,
> Feather white.
> Holds the image,
> On Hunter's Night.
> Angels called,
> For protection.
> Safeguard spell,
> With perfection.
> Blessed spirits,
> Surround in blue.
> Safe and sound,
> Heaven's view.
> Husk of corn,
> Feather white,
> Protect this person,
> On Hunter's Night.
> So Mote It Be.

NINETEEN
The Laughing Moon

Tiny magick of elf and faery,
Laughing Moon make joy and merry.
Toasting wishes of good health,
Embracing the white winter wealth.

The Full Moon in December is known as The Laughing Moon. This is a time to perform rituals dealing with success, prosperity, bounty, birds, new beginnings, New Year blessings and wishes, laughing, happiness, harmony, parents, nature, winter faeries, wishes in general, hopes, dreams, time capsules, generosity, and reincarnation. This is also a time to banish insomnia, stillness, and hopelessness.

The Time Tomb

Coven Ritual (Rainbow Magick)
by Sister Moon

MAGICKAL INTENTION: Creating a time capsule for the next generation of Witches.

TIME: Full Moon in December, Mars hour

TOOLS: One red candle, Frankincense oil, Myrrh incense, a gold box, pieces of paper in each of the following colors: white, blue, yellow, pink, red, orange, green, purple, brown, and gold, small and inexpensive items that date the important things that happened this year, such as a calendar, a newspaper clipping, a magazine, an article of clothing, etc., pens, and a large piece of white paper.

INSTRUCTIONS: Anoint the candle with Frankincense oil. Light the candle and the incense. On the small piece of colored paper, write your Wiccan name. Recall all of the important things that occurred during the year. Write down each event on the paper of the appropriate color; for example, on the white paper, write down all of the things that were pure to you. On the blue paper, write down all of the things that were calming or protecting to you. Do this for each color. On the large white paper, write your projections and predictions for the coming year. Roll the colored paper into scrolls and place them in the gold box along with the newspaper clippings and other paraphernalia. All hold hands, and recite the incantation. Bury the gold box, marking the spot so you will be able to dig it up the next year. When you dig it up, burn the scrolls of colored paper without rereading them and replace them with the new ones. The large white parchment should be reviewed each year before burning to see if your predictions and goals have come true. Burning these signify the movement and progress of life.

INCANTATION:

> December Moon recalls this year,
> All the laughter, all the tears.
> Bless the memories and lessons learned,
> Enhance the future with colors burned.
> Goddess and God and angels divine,
> Thank you for the year that shined.
> Weaving sisters of the colors band,
> Unite the power from hand to hand.
> Bond as family for eternity,
> Knitting together with certainty.
> Sisters and family bless the year,
> Unite in magick, joy and cheer.
> So Mote It Be.

The Success Spell

Solitary Ritual (Gold)
by Raiya

MAGICKAL INTENTION: To increase success in a specific endeavor. (To be performed outside in a fire-safe environment.)

TIME: Full Moon in December, Mars hour

TOOLS: One small gold candle, Success oil, Success incense, a pen with gold ink, a small square of gold parchment, a generous pinch of ginger, three dried clovers with three leaves.

INSTRUCTIONS: Anoint the candle with Success oil. Light the candle and the incense. On the gold parchment, write down what you wish to be successful in. Face south and recite the incantation. Crumble the three dried clovers with the ginger and sprinkle them into the burning incense. Recite the incantation again. Fold the parchment into a triangle and anoint each corner with the oil. Set the paper alight with the flame of the gold candle and allow it to burn with the incense. Recite the incantation one final time.

INCANTATION:

> A bit of ginger and clover nine,
> Guarantees success will be mine.
> Let the energy within be the key,
> To achieve my goal successfully.
> Little candle of golden light,
> Bring me my wish I ask this night.
> The act of burning calls to the south,
> May the fire of success never burn out.
> So Mote It Be.

○ ◑ ● ◐ ○

Undiscovered Joys

Solitary or Coven Ritual (Blue/Purple)
by Ambrosia

MAGICKAL INTENTION: To aid you in remembering your past life.

TIME: Full Moon in December, Moon hour

TOOLS: One blue candle and one purple candle for each participant, Beneficial Dream oil, Moon oil, Psychic incense, a large chalice, ten ounces of grape Kool-Aid, two ounces of apple juice, three
ice cubes, and an aquamarine.

INSTRUCTIONS: Anoint the blue candles with Beneficial Dream
oil. Anoint the purple candles with Moon oil. Light the candles
and the incense. Each participant should sit between their two
candles. Mix the grape Kool-Aid, apple juice, ice cubes, and aquamarine in the chalice. Pass the brew through the incense smoke.
Pour everyone a small amount of the brew. Everyone should drink
the brew and recite the incantation. Visualize yourself going back
into time. Feel the identity of who you were. Absorb every energy
and detail about your past you are able to.

INCANTATION:
>Send me back in time,
>Leaving this existence behind.
>Discover lives, experiences, loves, and
>>pains,
>
>Awaken me to the past as the wet rain.
>Of this Witches brew hits the stomach,
>And sends the mind down a past track.
>Lift my young, yet old heart to the sky,
>As the joy of discovering past lives lets
>>me fly.
>
>So Mote It Be.

Giggle Juice

Solitary or Coven Ritual (Yellow)
by Lyra

MAGICKAL INTENTION: To give the gift of laughter and joy.

TIME: Full Moon in December, Sun hour

TOOLS: One yellow candle, Easy Life oil, Happiness incense, one apple, one apricot, nine cherries, one peach, one plum, one cooking pot large enough to hold all of the ingredients, a minimum of one quart of apple cider (you can substitute sweet white wine if you wish), and cups or mason jars with lids.

INSTRUCTIONS: Anoint the candle with Easy Life oil. Light the candle and the incense. Pass each piece of fruit through the incense smoke. Peal and cut the fruit. Place it in the large pot and add a giggle. (You must think of a supremely happy thought to make the giggle pass from you to your brew.) Pass the cider or wine through the incense smoke and pour it into the large pot with all of the fruit. Put the pot on the stove and allow the liquid to come to a slight boil; simmer for exactly thirty-three minutes. Recite the incantation over the brew. Place the brew into the mason jars or cups to share with others.

INCANTATION:
> In this pot, I will brew,
> The gift of laughter to share with you.
> With fruits so sublime,
> Ahhh! A nectar divine!
> Giggles, laughs, and merriment abound,
> I'll add to this brew the happiest sounds.

Bring laughter and joy to all who drink,
The gift I give with giggles and wink.
So Mote It Be.

○ ◑ ● ◐ ○

Reflections

Solitary Ritual (Gold)
by Poseidon

MAGICKAL INTENTION: A ritual to help New Year's wishes and resolutions come true.

TIME: Full Moon in December, Sun hour

TOOLS: One large gold candle, Cleomay oil, Sweet Clover incense, a bad picture of yourself, one pen with gold ink, and a good picture of yourself.

INSTRUCTIONS: Anoint the candle with Cleomay oil. Light the candle and incense. Write in gold on the front of the bad picture four things that keep you from your goals and from succeeding in your New Year's resolutions. On the good picture, write down four things you want to change for the coming year and four reasons why you want to succeed. Pass the bad picture in widdershins motion through the incense smoke, and place it on the left side of your bathroom mirror. Pass the good picture in deosil motion through the incense smoke, and recite the incantation. Place the good picture on the right side of the bathroom mirror. When you see these pictures, the spell will work its magick to keep you on track and focused.

INCANTATION:

> Last full moon of the year,
> A change has come, that is clear.
> Image to image, it is pressed,
> Upon the reflecting looking glass.
> I know I can, I know I will,
> Reach my goals of wishes fulfilled.
> No longer sad of what is not,
> I focus now on what I want.
> I see this face every day,
> Smiling and happy is how I'll stay.
> I take pride as I succeed,
> And I love what I achieve.
> So Mote It Be.

○ ◑ ● ◑ ○

Sights Unseen

Solitary Ritual (Pink, Purple, and Blue)
by Leebrah

MAGICKAL INTENTION: To speak with the winter faeries and gather information from them.

TIME: Full Moon in December, Venus hour

TOOLS: A container of salt, Special Favors oils, Venus and Peace incenses, an incense burner, one pink candle, one purple candle, one blue candle, a faery statue, and one small bag of faery dust.

INSTRUCTIONS: Draw a circle of salt big enough for you to sit and relax in. Place the incenses in the burner and light the incenses. Anoint the candles with the Special Favors oil. Place the candles inside the circle in a triangle shape. Light the candles. Pass the faery statue through the incense smoke in deosil motion three times. Place the faery statue in the middle of the circle. Recite the incantation and sprinkle the faery dust over the statue. Listen and watch. The winter faeries have a subtle way of getting their information to you.

INCANTATION:

> Light as a feather, flying through the air,
> Show me your magick, let me know you're there.
> Tip-toe into my circle white,
> Let me see you upon this night.
> Winter faery come to me, and show me the sights unseen,
> I will open my eyes, with love in my heart.
> To any and all information that you will part.
> My God and Goddess shall see, this is my will,
> So Mote It Be.

○ ◑ ● ◑ ○

Banking Notes

Solitary or Coven Ritual (Green)
by Daughter of Dragons

MAGICKAL INTENTION: To gain prosperity in your life.

TIME: Full Moon in December, Jupiter hour

TOOLS: One green candle, Jade oil, Prosperity incense, your bills, and your checkbook.

INSTRUCTIONS: Anoint the candle with Jade oil. Light the candle and the incense. Pass each of your bills widdershins through the incense smoke. Write checks out for your bills. On the memo portion of each of your checks, write these symbols:

They are translated as "dough back to me." Recite the incantation and pass each check in deosil motion through the incense smoke. Write the symbols on every check you write for one solid year and watch your prosperity grow.

INCANTATION:

> Musical notes will sing,
> Prosperity will ring.
> Return tenfold to me,
> Wealth and prosperity.
> So Mote It Be.

TWENTY
Yule

Elks will bugle at the night tree,
Nibbling the gifts of breads and seed.
Yuletide wishes on the smallest night,
To bring back the sun, bring back the light.

Yule is on December 21 or December 22 and is a minor Sabbat. It's also the shortest day of the year. This is a time to perform rituals dealing with enlightenment, awakening, intelligence, generosity, gifts, attraction, wild animals, contentment, love, wealth, charms, prosperity, protection, fertility, empathy, mothers in general, and gratitude. This is also a time to honor the God and Goddess in their three phases.

Creature Comforts

Solitary or Coven Ritual (Brown)
by Indigo

MAGICKAL INTENTION: To feed the hungry wildlife.

TIME: December 21 or 22, Sun hour

TOOLS: One brown candle, Witching Well incense, Witching Well oil, a handful of pinecones, a jar of peanut butter, a bag of birdseed, a large bowl, two cups of whole oats, two cups of whole wheat, two cups of whole dried corn, two cups of dried apple, and two cups of dark molasses.

INSTRUCTIONS: Anoint the candle with the oil. Light the candle and the incense. Cover the pinecones with peanut butter. Roll the peanut-buttered pinecone in the birdseed to coat. Set aside. In a large bowl, combine the oats, wheat, corn, and dried apple pieces. Add the molasses and mix well. Recite the incantation.

Take the pinecones and grain mixture to a place where wildlife congregate, and leave it at the base of a tree. Sprinkle the area with a handful of the mixture to attract the animals. Recite the incantation once again.

Do not leave this offering too close to civilization, as we do not want to encourage the wildlife to be dependent on humans for food. You can do the same spell for homeless domestic animals by taking dog or cat food to your local animal shelter.

INCANTATION:

> To the creatures great and small,
> With our love, protect them all.
> Surround them with the Goddess light,

Shroud them on this winter night.
Offer them health and hearty feed,
Let this gift cure their basic need.
Our wonderful creatures in the wild,
Bless this winter to be warm and mild.
So Mote It Be.

○ ◐ ● ◑ ○

The Harmony Exchange

Coven Ritual (Yellow)
by Sister Moon

MAGICKAL INTENTION: To exchange magickal gifts with the other Coven members.

TIME: December 21 or 22, Jupiter hour. This ritual needs to be held outside in a natural setting near a pine tree.

TOOLS: Red candles for half of the participants, green candles for the other half, White Solstice oil, White Solstice incense, a small gift for each participant (see Note), a star for the top of the tree (make it out of something birds or animals can eat), twelve offerings of food for the wild animals, hot cocoa or cider, and a cup for each participant. Note: The gifts for the participants should be inexpensive, and should be something magickal such as a talisman or amulet, a tapestry, jewelry, tarot cards, and so on. Make sure the gift is wrapped and can be suspended from a tree branch.

INSTRUCTIONS: Anoint all of the candles with the White Solstice oil. Light the candles and the incense. Tie each gift on a branch of the tree. Place the star on the top of the tree. Place the twelve food items at the tree's base. Pour the cocoa or cider into the cups, each participant make a toast, and drink. All hold hands, recite the incantation, and circle halfway around the tree. One by one, each Witch closes her eyes and selects a gift from the tree. (She can simply point in the direction of the nearest gift and it can then be retrieved.) Recite the incantation again and leave the area.

INCANTATION:

> Goddess divine, mother of child,
> We offer our gifts to the creatures of wild.
> In your name we honor the solstice of Yule,
> We celebrate your love and the Wiccan rule.
> Goddess divine, our heavenly mother,
> We offer our gifts to our sisters and brothers.
> In your name, we honor life and earth,
> And all of nature that you gave birth.
> So Mote It Be.

Nova's Yule Celebration

Solitary or Coven Ritual (Red)
by Nova

MAGICKAL INTENTION: To celebrate the rebirth of the God at Yule.

TIME: December 21 or 22, Moon hour

TOOLS: Seven red candles, six green candles, While Solstice oil, and White Solstice incense.

INSTRUCTIONS: Place the candles in a circle. Anoint the candles with White Solstice oil. Light the candles and the incense. Stand in the middle of the circle and recite the incantation. Then dance around the outside of the circle in thirteen rotations with arms outstretched to the sky.

INCANTATION:

Celebration of the Moon,
As I recite this magickal tune.
The God is reborn today on Yule,
He will act as our energy fuel.
To light the fires within,
And to us lend,
A desire, a love, and a passion,
For this pure-hearted religion.
This is my will, So Mote It Be.

The Yule Log

Solitary or Coven Ritual (Red/White)
by Ambrosia

MAGICKAL INTENTION: To bless and protect the home.

TIME: December 21 or 22, Mars hour

TOOLS: A fireplace, one red candle, one white candle, Moonlight oil, a Yule log, Dragon's Blood ink, a handful of juniper berries, and nine ivy leaves.

INSTRUCTIONS: Light a fire in the fireplace. Anoint both of the candles with the Moonlight oil and place them on either side of the fireplace. Using the Dragon's Blood ink, draw Wiccan symbols (such as pentagrams, moons, etc.) on the Yule log. Then write the words "Bless this home." Place the Yule log in the flames. Cast in the juniper berries and ivy leaves while reciting the incantation.

INCANTATION:

> A blessing written in Dragon's Blood,
> To surround our home with protection and love.
> A dash of ivy, a dusting of juniper berries,
> Flying into the flame like blessing faeries.
> A log consumed by the Yule flame,
> Sprinkling a blessing on this home like rain.
> Bless our lives with each flame that sparks,
> And keep us safe in the light and the dark.
> So Mote It Be.

Prosperous Home

Solitary Ritual (Green/Blue)
by Aquila Eagle

MAGICKAL INTENTION: To bring prosperity and protection into the home.

TIME: December 21 or 22, Moon hour

TOOLS: Prosperity, Coins in a Fountain, and Tranquillity incenses, four incense burners, one tablespoon each of chives, eucalyptus, gourd, and Irish moss, a bowl, Bayberry and Protection oils, four small mojos, and one green candle.

INSTRUCTIONS: Combine the incenses and then divide them among the four incense burners. Combine all of the herbs in the bowl and add two drops of each oil into the mixture; stir well. Divide the herb mixture among the four mojo bags. Anoint the candle with both oils. Light the candle and the incenses. Pass the mojo bags in deosil motion through the incense smoke.

Go to the lowest level of your home, and place the incense burners in the four farthest corners in each direction. Place the four mojos in the highest level of your home in the four most distant corners.

Go to a place in your home between those two levels, and recite the incantation. Visualize money pouring into every door and window of your home. Visualize your home with a solid blue aura issuing from it. When the spell has been cast, bury the four mojo bags outside of your home in the four directions. Prosperity and protection will abound for a full year.

INCANTATION:

Corner to corner, this house all around,
Bring good fortune and prosperity abound!
Within these walls, the magick protects,
Our daily lives as we project.
Guide the flow of energy to be,
A place of protection and prosperity.
Come together to guard and give,
Abundance to us as we live.
So Mote It Be.

○ ◐ ● ◑ ○

Angel on My Shoulder

Solitary or Coven Ritual (Purple/Blue)
by Indigo

MAGICKAL INTENTION: To meet your Guardian Angel.

TIME: December 21 or 22, Sunset

TOOLS: One blue candle, one purple candle, Angel oil, Vision incense, a red flannel mojo, seven pinches of lemongrass, thirteen magnolia petals, seven Job's tears, and three pinches of salt.

INSTRUCTIONS: Anoint both candles with Angel oil. Light the candle and the incense. Place in the mojo the lemongrass, magnolia petals, Job's tears, and salt. Add three drops of Angel oil and seal the mojo. Tie the strings in three knots and pass the mojo in deosil motion through the incense smoke while reciting the incantation. Keep the mojo with you, and your Guardian Angel will reveal her or himself to you soon.

INCANTATION:

> Guardian Angel that watches me,
> I ask for your image now to see.
> I conjure an offering on this night,
> Yuletide greetings Angel bright.
> So Mote It Be.

○ ◐ ● ◑ ○

A Cool Yule

Solitary Ritual (Blue)
by Sister Moon

MAGICKAL INTENTION: To have contentment of the heart.

TIME: December 21 or 22, Venus hour

TOOLS: Three blue candles, Peace oil, Tranquillity incense, a blazing fire in a fireplace, a found feather, a pinch of earth, and a pinch of snow.

INSTRUCTIONS: Anoint the candles with the Peace oil. Light the candles and the incense. Sit before the fire and place the candles and the incense on the hearth. Visualize everything that you are thankful for. After you think of everything that gives you a sense of peace, recite the incantation. Throw the feather, earth, and snow into the fire. Your contentment will last a full year.

INCANTATION:

> The shortest day,
> Of the year.
> A time to pray,
> A time of cheer.
> Thankful for,
> A contented heart.
> That beats with peace,
> From light to dark.
> An offering of,
> The elements of earth.
> A token of love,
> Granting mirth.

Blessed be,
This Yule's day.
Tranquil soul,
Thankful ways.
So Mote It Be.

TWENTY-ONE
The Blue Moon

○ ◑ ● ◕ ○

Link the hands in circles round,
'Tis the time to draw the Moon down.
Cast the magick from a bird's-eye view,
When the Moon is full and when it's Blue.

A second Full Moon in one month is known as The Blue Moon. This is the time to perform rituals dealing with special favors and blessings, rededication of life and purpose, completion, any magick involving heights, love, prosperity, good health, wishes and fantasies that need to become realities, psychic abilities, cleansing the altar and the tools, renewing life energy, control, and disguises. This is also a time to banish ego problems, identity problems, and disagreements in general.

By the Light of the Moon

Solitary Ritual (White)
by Ariel

MAGICKAL INTENTION: To cleanse all ritual tools and to renew them by the infusion of the intense energy of the Blue Moon.

TIME: Blue Moon, Moon hour.

TOOLS: All of your magickal tools including your divining tools and stones, one white candle, Mist oil, and Amulet incense.

INSTRUCTIONS: Cleanse a circle around your altar. Place all of your tools on the altar. Anoint the candle with Mist oil. Light the candle and the incense. Pass each tool through the incense smoke in deosil motion three times while reciting the incantation. Place all of the tools outside to be bathed in the light of the full moon so they will absorb its energy. Make sure you retrieve your tools before sunrise. Place them in a quiet, dark place for three nights. Your tools are now cleansed and recharged by an enormous power.

INCANTATION:
> Mighty Blue Moon, thirteenth of year,
> Energize my tools with light and sear.
> Infuse these provisions that are used and worn,
> Make them new by quake of morn.
> Mighty Blue Moon, bright orb above,
> Radiate your power with light and love.
> Concentration and endowment of skill,
> By the light of the moon, empower my will.
> So Mote It Be.

○ ◑ ● ◐ ○

The Mighty Sword

Coven or Solitary Ritual (Green)
by Crystal Ball

MAGICKAL INTENTION: To win the lottery.

TIME: Blue Moon, Sun hour

TOOLS: Three green candles, Magnet oil, Prosperity incense, a cauldron, seven pumpkin seeds, a piece of ginger root, a pinch of cinnamon, two pinches of basil, a snip of plantain, three pieces of Devil's Shoestring, a large sword, and your lottery ticket game board (a ticket you use to select your numbers—if you usually play "quick pick," you just use a blank board).

INSTRUCTIONS: Anoint the candles with Magnet oil. Place three heaping teaspoons of incense in the cauldron. Light the candles and the incense. Place all of the seeds and herbs into the cauldron. Rest the sword across the cauldron's mouth on the rim. Carefully place the lottery game board on the sword. Recite the incantation and allow the ticket to sit in the incense smoke over the cauldron for about five minutes. When the spell is complete, take your game board to your lottery cashier to place your bet. Scatter the ashes on the earth before the drawing takes place.

INCANTATION:

> With the help of the mighty sword,
> Lend me your powers, Lady and Lord.
> The tide has turned; my numbers will win,
> Lottery, lottery, wealth transcend!

Sword and cauldron balancing numbers,
Now awake from sleeping slumber.
Dance and jump right from the pot,
Winning this lottery is my lot!
So Mote It Be.

○ ◑ ● ◗ ○

The Blue Brew

Coven Ritual (Blue/Purple)
by Sister Moon

MAGICKAL INTENTION: To make one specific fantasy come true.

TIME: Blue Moon, Jupiter hour

TOOLS: One blue candle, Blue Moon oil and incense, one large chalice, twelve ouces of blue margarita mix, a squeeze of lime, five ice cubes, one turquoise, a dash of grenadine, a blue feather, an athame, and a small cup for each participant.

INSTRUCTIONS: Anoint the candle with the oil. Light the candle and the incense. Concentrate on a fantasy that you would really like to come true. (The fantasy should be limited to one major component.) Visualize that specific element and see it in your third eye. In the large chalice combine the blue margarita mix, lime juice, ice cubes, turquoise, and grenadine. Recite the incantation as you visualize your fantasy. Stir the brew in deosil motion with the feather. With the athame, draw a pentagram over the chalice. Pass the brew through the incense. Pour a small amount of brew into each participant's cup. Everyone should drink the brew at the exact time while visualizing their fantasy.

INCANTATION:

> Gathered beneath a Moon of Blue,
> A spell is cast in a Witch's brew.
> A splash of potion of aqua flavor,
> Add with fire and blood to savor.
> Stone of wisdom and water frozen,
> Creates the reality of what I've chosen.
> Stir with wings in deosil fashion,
> Unlocks the truth of Witch's passion.
> *"Ala Luna Aqua Zar,"*
> Five points of the magickal star.
> Water, earth, fire and air,
> Spirit invoked from this prayer.
> Blue smoke circles and encompass thee,
> Make my dream a reality.
> Once upon this Moon so blue,
> Grant my wish within this brew.
> So Mote It Be.

The Angel Scarf

Solitary or Coven Ritual (White)
by Nova

MAGICKAL INTENTION: To summon the Angels for protection or guidance.

TIME: Blue Moon, Sun hour

TOOLS: Five white candles, Holy Smoke oil, Angel Blessing incense, and a white scarf.

INSTRUCTIONS: Place the candles in a circle. Anoint them with Holy Smoke oil. Place the incense in the middle of the circle and sit next to it. Light the candles and the incense. Pass the scarf in deosil motion through the incense smoke while reciting the incantation. Continue passing the scarf through the incense smoke until you feel the scarf has been blessed. Wear the scarf when you need protection or guidance.

INCANTATION:

> Guardian Angels I call on thee,
> Hear my summons and come to me.
> I ask for a blessing of light,
> On this scarf of pure white.
> Please grant to me protection and
>   guidance,
> In actions of destiny's unfolding
>   chance.
> A truly blessed Witch would I be,
> If you would send aid to me.
> When in future need,
> A wearing of this scarf will heed.
> The blessing from this day,
> And aid in dark and the sun's ray.
> So Mote It Be.

○ ◑ ● ◑ ○

Two Moons

Solitary or Coven Ritual (Blue)
by Sister Moon

MAGICKAL INTENTION: To fulfill your dreams.

TIME: The components of this spell are performed at two different times: the first full moon of the month, Jupiter hour, and the Blue Moon, Jupiter hour

TOOLS: Two blue candles, Blue Moon oil and incense, two glass bottles with airtight corks or lids, blue parchment, blue ink, 14 Job's tears, two fishing bobbers, fishing line, and a large body of water.

INSTRUCTIONS: On the first Full Moon of the month, Jupiter hour, light the Blue Moon incense. Write in blue ink on the blue parchment a wish that comes from your heart. It needs to be specific and it cannot be as generic as "a lot of money" or "win the lottery." Anoint the parchment with the Blue Moon oil and place it in one of the bottles along with seven of the Job's tears. Pass the bottle through the incense smoke.

Tie some fishing line on the bottle and add a bobber. Recite the incantation and throw the bottle into the body of water, but tie one end of the fishing line to something stationary on shore.

On the Blue Moon, Jupiter hour, repeat the same process, but this time make your wish something that will affect a lot of people. Throw the second bottle into the same water and tie it to another stationary object on shore.

Upon the following full moon, retrieve the two bottles (that is, if they are still there). If one or both are there, unstopper the bottle and burn the parchment. Bury the ashes in a hole along with the Job's tears. The wishes will come true within a year.

However, if one or both of the bottles are gone, your wish will come true within a moon's cycle.

INCANTATION:

> Two moons in the lunar rise,
> One white, one blue, light the skies.
> Wishes cast into the well,
> Of the waters that dance and swell.
> Seven tears of Job reside,
> Beneath the water's ebb and tide.
> Waiting for the wish to flow,
> Into my life, they shall go.
> Goddess of the earth and water,
> Bestow the wishes of your daughter.
> Grant this vision that I see,
> This is my will, So Mote It Be.

Pretty Bird Wants a Cracker

Solitary Ritual (Black/White)
by Poseidon

MAGICKAL INTENTION: To overcome an enemy or obsession.

TIME: Blue Moon, Saturn hour

TOOLS: One black candle, Black Musk oil, Banishing incense, a jar of molasses, and a box of saltines.

INSTRUCTIONS: Anoint the candle with Black Musk oil. Light the candle and the incense. Condense the negative energy that you are experiencing to one word or one name. With the molasses, write each letter of the word on a cracker until the entire word is spelled out. Recite the incantation over the crackers, crumble them, and toss them into your front yard. Recite the incantation again over the crumbs. As the birds scoop them up, they will take away the problem.

INCANTATION:

Sticky sweet letters are scribed,
Feathered fowls take the bribe.
Upon the bread made for birds,
A riddance discarded in one word.
Feathered friend, pick the scatter,
Let me hear your feasting chatter.
Molasses makes the bread so sweet,
As my enemy now retreats.
Exit from life and mind,
Your torture now forever blind.
Feathered friends gather and feast,
Of an obsession that is now deceased.
So Mote It Be.

The Real Me

Solitary or Coven Ritual (Rainbow)
by Leebrah

MAGICKAL INTENTION: To promote self-confidence.

TIME: Blue Moon, any hour

TOOLS: One rainbow-colored candle, Positive Attitude oil, a pinch each of barley, aloe, curry, hydrangea, lavender, walnut, and beet, a mortar and pestle, Obsidian incense, Aura Cleansing, Peace, Positive Attitude, Lovely, Black Cat, Be Mine, Good luck, and Pharaoh oils, a kyanite, and one red flannel mojo.

INSTRUCTIONS: Anoint the candle with Positive Attitude oil. Light the candle and the incense. Combine and crush all herbs and three drops of each of the oils together in the mortar. Visualize your self-confidence glowing about you in a colorful aura. Imagine it becoming brighter and brighter. Place the mixture along with the stone in the red flannel mojo. Recite the incantation and pass the mojo in deosil motion through the incense smoke. Carry the mojo with you when you need to promote your self-confidence.

INCANTATION:

> Shoulders back, head held high,
> Eye contact, without a sigh.
> No questions of, "Did I do that right?"
> "Am I good enough?" There will be no fight!
> I am myself, I am whole today.
> No more bad thoughts will come my way.
> I am confident that I will do it right,
> And I am good enough without a fight.
> My God and Goddess, I thank thee,
> This is my will, So Mote It Be.

TWENTY-TWO

Friday the Thirteenth, Waxing Moon

Waxing Friday, number thirteen!
Familiars dance with tambourines!
Mortals fear the moonlit mist,
Witches welcome the haunting bliss.

Friday the Thirteenth beneath the waxing moon is a magickal time indeed! As the Full Moon has unpredictable power, so does the waxing moon on Friday the Thirteenth. Witches in general are energized by this day and are more joyful than usual by night. This is the time to perform rituals dealing with familiars, divining, love magick, sex magick, control, uncovering secrets, finding lost treasures, honoring Witches of past and present, personal gratification, popularity, self-confidence, and haunting on any level.

The Stone Pillow

Coven or Solitary Ritual (Purple)
by Colleechee

MAGICKAL INTENTION: To uncover a secret.

TIME: Friday the thirteenth, Waxing Moon, Mercury hour

TOOLS: One purple candle, Lily of the Valley oil, Wolf incense, a bloodstone, an agate, and a red flannel mojo.

INSTRUCTIONS: Anoint the candle with the Lily of the Valley oil. Light the candle and the incense. Place the stones in the mojo and pass it in deosil motion ten times through the incense smoke while reciting the incantation. Place the mojo beneath your pillow. Before going to sleep, ask out loud the question to which you want to know the answer. The answer will be revealed to you in your dreams.

INCANTATION:

Pillow of stones,
Beneath my head,
Reveal the tones
Of words unsaid.
Question no more,
I need to know.
Dreams will pour,
My mind will flow.
So Mote It Be.

○ ◐ ● ◑ ○

Under My Spell

Solitary Ritual (Purple)
by Sister Moon

MAGICKAL INTENTION: To have complete control over a specific situation.

TIME: Friday the Thirteenth, Waxing Moon, Mars hour

TOOLS: Three purple candles, Controlling oil, Controlling incense, a floating incense burner, a pinch of High John the Conqueror, a purple balloon, purple parchment, a pan with purple ink, string, helium, and a body of water (bathtub, hot tub, or lake is fine).

INSTRUCTIONS: Anoint the candles with Controlling oil. Light the candles and place them near the water. Place the incense in the floating incense burner and light it. Place the High John herb into the balloon. On the purple parchment write down exactly what situation you desire to have complete control over. Be specific. Roll the parchment into a scroll and insert it into the balloon. Inflate the balloon with the helium and tie it with the string. Visualize the situation turning out exactly as you want it to. Holding the balloon by the string, get into the water. Allow the balloon to rise and hover over the incense. Still holding the balloon string, submerge yourself in the water beneath the incense burner so that it and the balloon are over your head. Recite the incantation while you are under the water. Let go of the balloon and allow it to drift away without controlling it. Your control spell is now underway.

INCANTATION:
> Over my head and in the air,
> High John the Conqueror controls the pair.

Beneath the water, a Witch reflects,
All the control with complete respect.
So Mote It Be.

○ ◐ ● ◑ ○

Chocolate Kisses

Solitary Ritual (Pink)
by Astra

MAGICKAL INTENTION: To awaken feelings of intense love between a couple.

TIME: Friday the Thirteenth, Waxing Moon, Venus hour

TOOLS: Two pink candles, Lovers oil, Venus incense, one or two bags of Hershey's Kisses, a fondue pot, one teaspoon of vanilla, one teaspoon of cinnamon, two bananas, a fresh pineapple or canned chunk pineapple, a container of raspberries, a container of strawberries, and one bouquet of daisies. (Feel free to substitute any fruit you like.)

INSTRUCTIONS: This spell creates a chocolate fondue for you and your lover. Anoint the candles with Lovers oil. Light the candles and the incense. Place the Kisses in the fondue pot and allow them to melt slowly. Add the vanilla and cinnamon into the melting chocolate, while reciting Incantation One. Cut the fruit into bite-size pieces and place on a tray. While cutting the fruit, recite Incantation Two. Set the fruit, chocolate, and daisies onto a table. Sit down with your loved one and take turns feeding each other the chocolate-covered fruit. Take the time to enjoy this very special spell.

INCANTATION ONE:

> I place these herbs of love within my heart's
> chocolate.
> Knowing that warmth within my soul will be relit,
> I stir the chocolate as a stir of emotions begins to
> be reborn.
> So Mote It Be.

INCANTATION TWO:

> With each slice of nature's candy,
> A slice of negativity is taken from our connection.
> The sweet taste of sugar upon your soft lips,
> Will strengthen our affection.
> The earth's daisies touch our hearts,
> Like the sun rays reach our souls.
> The rebirth of our love
> Is being celebrated here today.
> So Mote It Be.

○ ◑ ● ◐ ○

Spirits and Sprites

Coven or Solitary Ritual (Yellow/Purple)
by Journey

MAGICKAL INTENTION: To attract the psychic influence of a good spirit in order to answer a question.

TIME: Friday the Thirteenth, Waxing Moon, Venus hour

TOOLS: One yellow candle, one purple candle, Psychic oil, Spirit Guide incense, one teaspoon of dried lavender, one tablespoon of sandalwood, a mortar and pestle, one red flannel mojo, and a small piece of jasper.

INSTRUCTIONS: Anoint both candles with Psychic oil. Light the candles and the incense. Combine the lavender and sandalwood in the mortar. Place the herbs in the mojo with the jasper. Anoint the mojo with Psychic oil and pass it in deosil motion through the incense smoke three times while reciting the incantation. Ask your question out loud. Wait for your message from the good spirit. Don't forget to thank the spirit for the information you receive.

INCANTATION:

> Spirit speak, Spirit teach,
> As incense burns, Spirit reach.
> You may do good, as well you
>   should,
> If not, stay there if you would.
> Spirit wise, Spirit good,
> Do you have a message for me?
> Lavender will help me see.
> And sandalwood and jasper,
> To help me capture,
> The words of wisdom I am after.
> So Mote It Be.

○ ◑ ● ◐ ○

Going for the Gold

Solitary or Coven Ritual (Green, Gold and Blue)
by Leebrah

MAGICKAL INTENTION: To find something that may be lost or find new treasures.

TIME: Friday the Thirteenth, Waxing Moon, Mercury hour

TOOLS: One green candle, Isis and Blue Moon oils, Good Luck, Fast Luck, and Coins in the Fountain incenses, one teaspoon each of bamboo, bluebell, and pecan, a mortar and pestle, one green fern, potting soil, and new pot for the plant.

INSTRUCTIONS: Anoint the candle with the oils. Light the candles and the incenses. Combine the herbs in the mortar and crush with the pestle. Loosen the soil around the roots of the fern. Place new soil in the pot and add the crushed herbs. Add three drops of each oil into the soil. Pass the potted plant in deosil motion through the incense smoke while reciting the appropriate incantation. Place your plant in a special place in your home to bring the treasures to you. This spell also helps you to keep from losing treasures in the future.

INCANTATION TO FIND A LOST ITEM:
>I have lost you, please come to me,
>My memory slips and passes, you see.
>Help me find what I have lost,
>Please do this at no cost.
>Precious item that is misplaced,
>Present yourself in urgent haste.
>In advance, I thank thee.
>This is my will, So Mote It Be.

INCANTATION TO FIND NEW TREASURES:
> A new treasure is what I long to find,
> With help from thee, I do not mind.
> I only ask for what I deserve,
> No more, no less, and throw no curves.
> Treasures that are special in ways,
> That makes Friday Thirteenth a memorable day.
> Please let it stay around, you see,
> This is my will, So Mote It Be.

○ ◑ ● ◑ ○

Message in a Flower

Solitary or Coven Ritual (Purple/Gold)
by Raiya

MAGICKAL INTENTION: A ritual to honor the Witches of the past.

TIME: Friday the Thirteenth, Waxing Moon, Moon hour

TOOLS: One purple candle, one gold candle, Magick oil, Magick incense, the following flowers for a bouquet: yarrow, dandelion, carnation, Indian paintbrush, morning glory, lily, and iris, and a piece of gold ribbon as long as you are tall plus three inches more.

INSTRUCTIONS: Cast your circle in a secluded area near a fast-flowing body of water. Anoint the candles with the Magick oil. Light the candles and the incense. Arrange the flowers in a bouquet. Wrap the gold ribbon around the bottom three inches of the stems. Tie the loose ends of the ribbon in a knot or bow. Hold the bouquet above your head with both hands and recite the incantation. Gently place the bouquet in the water and send it on its way.

INCANTATION:

> To my sisters and brothers that came before,
> I thank you for keeping an open door.
> And for teaching others the sacred ways,
> We honor you through the end of our days.
> Through the water we send the gift of flowers,
> For this earth is great because of your powers.
> We honor you all for the magick of old,
> That brought us to this land of gold.
> So Mote It Be.

The Shining Pentacles

Solitary Ritual (Purple/Gold)
by Sister Moon

MAGICKAL INTENTION: To have great personal powers and awesome magick.

TIME: Friday the Thirteenth, Waxing Moon, Moon hour

TOOLS: Two purple candles, one gold candle, Double Action oil, Double Action incense, your cingula, your cape, one gold pentagram necklace, one silver pentagram necklace, and one small pyramid. You will need to perform this ritual in an open field in total privacy.

INSTRUCTIONS: Anoint the three candles with Double Action oil. Light the candles and the incense. Place the candles in a triangle. Place the incense in the center of the triangle. Place the gold pentagram beside the gold candle. Place the silver pentagram beside one purple candle. Place the pyramid beside the other purple candle. Skyclad, except for cape and cingula, stand inside the three-candle triangle and allow the incense to rise up through your cape. Recite the incantation. Place both pentagram necklaces around your neck and leave them on until the next Full Moon.

INCANTATION:

> Within the smoke my power takes,
> A double surge within its wake.
> Rise with strength into the folds,
> Of my cape, belt, and soul.
> Shining pentacles in the trine,
> I beseech the powers of the divine.
> Gold and silver points of five,
> Make my powers come alive!
> Every drop of my blood,
> Receives the energy as it floods.
> Through my veins and out my pores,
> Thirteenth Friday, now double my score.
> So Mote It Be.

TWENTY-THREE

Fríday the Thirteenth, Waning Moon

Ebony crows perched at the gate,
Reciting spells they imitate.
Waning Friday, thirteenth night,
Lock the doors at twilight.

Friday the Thirteenth on a waning moon has mystical energies, but they are a bit more ominous than a waxing Friday the Thirteenth. Witches are more accident prone at this time. It is best to perform simple spells that do not involve other people. This is a time to perform rituals dealing with protection on all levels, past lives, to solidify escape paths, preparing amulets, finding familiars, divining the history of antiques, breaking hexes, exorcism, and purification. This is also a time to banish things that prevent you from succeeding.

Burn, Baby, Burn!

Coven or Solitary Ritual (Gray/Black)
by Crystal Ball

MAGICKAL INTENTION: To remove all negativity, obstacles, or negative forces that prevent you from being successful or from reaching your goals.

TIME: Friday the Thirteenth, Waning Moon, Mars hour

TOOLS: Thirteen black votive candles, JuJu oil, Exodus and Midnight incenses, a hibachi, thirteen pieces of self-starting charcoal, thirteen squares of gray parchment, thirteen small pinches of five finger grass (cinquefoil), a pen with black ink, a stone that weighs thirteen pounds, and an extra-large mojo.

INSTRUCTIONS: Anoint the thirteen votives with JuJu oil. Place the Midnight incense in the incense burner. Arrange the thirteen votives in a circle around the hibachi. Light the candles and the incense. Place the thirteen pieces of charcoal in the hibachi and sprinkle them with the Exodus incense. Light the incense on the charcoal. Sprinkle the five finger grass on the charcoal. Write on each piece of parchment something that prevents you from achieving your goals. If you cannot think of thirteen different things, write the same thing on each parchment. Roll each piece of parchment into a scroll and place the scrolls on the burning charcoal. Recite the incantation.

After the coals have turned to ash and are completely cool, place the ashes into the red mojo. Dig a hole that is west of where you live and place the mojo in the hole. Place the large stone over the mojo so it will never release the obstacles that are within it. Recite the incantation one more time and fill in the hole.

INCANTATION:

>With Midnight black as coal,
>For all evil the bell will toll.
>All the obstacles will not block,
>When success and wealth come to knock.
>Fear will not hesitate or stop me,
>Neither will anger nor jealousy.
>With the thirteenth Friday in its wane,
>Exodus burns the negativity and pain.
>So Mote It Be.

○ ◑ ● ◐ ○

Past Lives Retained

Solitary Ritual (Purple)
by Leebrah

MAGICKAL INTENTION: To bring back memories of past lives; to retain the information of mistakes made in the past so they will not be made again in this lifetime or future lifetimes.

TIME: Friday the Thirteenth, Waning Moon, Moon hour

TOOLS: Dove's Flight and Draw Across incenses, one purple candle, Moon oil, one clear calcite, a pen with black ink, a piece of white parchment, and two incense burners.

INSTRUCTIONS: Place the incenses into separate burners. Anoint the candle with the Moon oil. Light the candle and the incenses. Lie on the ground on your back and place the incense burners at either side of your head. Place the candle above your head, creating a triangle. Place the calcite stone on your third eye. Recite the incantation. As the information comes into your head, write down everything that is revealed to you. Review all that you have received and know where your mistakes were in the past. To avoid the mistakes in this lifetime, burn the parchment after you have memorized the lessons written there.

INCANTATION:

> Knowledge of past issues not retained,
> Make for a journey that remains the same.
> Bring forth the pieces of my former life,
> So my error is once, not twice.
> Protect me on this critical tour,
> When all has been shown, I will know the cure.
> Then bring me forward to the present day,
> Let the wisdom of lessons show me the way.
> So Mote It Be.

Harm's Way

Coven Ritual (Blue)
by Sister Moon

MAGICKAL INTENTION: Protection.

TIME: Friday the Thirteenth, Waning Moon, Saturn hour

TOOLS: Three blue candles, Protection oil, Protection incense, and a piece of rope from a hangman's noose.

INSTRUCTIONS: Anoint the candles with the oil. Light the candles and the incense. Visualize an aura of blue encompassing you. Ask the angels to keep each and every one of you safe from harm. Take a small strand of rope from the noose and cut it to fit your ankle or wrist. Pass the strand in deosil motion through the incense smoke and recite the incantation.

Wear the rope on your wrist or ankle during times of danger. If at any time the strand of rope begins to chafe or burn you, that is your warning that danger is near and to leave the area you are in.

INCANTATION:

> I summon the power of the mighty Zeus,
> To unleash the power of this noose.
> Around my body it is tied,
> For protection it now resides.
> Strand be smooth and do not chafe,
> Mighty Zeus, keep me safe.
> Protect me now night and day,
> Keep me from all of harm's way.
> So Mote It Be.

○ ◐ ● ◑ ○

True Blue Protection

Coven or Solitary Ritual (Blue)
by Ambrosia

MAGICKAL INTENTION: To keep enemies at bay.

TIME: Friday the Thirteenth, Waning Moon, late at night when no one is around.

TOOLS: One blue candle, Lotus oil, Protection incense, an athame, and salt.

INSTRUCTIONS: Make sure this spell is done late at night and no one is near your residence. Anoint the candle with the oil. Light the candle and the incense. Recite the incantation. While saying, "North, South, East, and West," point in those directions with the athame. Liberally sprinkle the salt in deosil motion around the outside of your residence.

INCANTATION:

> Under darkness of night's sky,
> While Friday the Thirteenth's moon is high.
> North, south, east and west,
> Protection in all areas is best.
> With a sprinkling of salt to keep enemies at bay,
> Banish all those evil-minded far away.
> Let true blue burn bright,
> And protect in its shining light.
> So Mote It Be.

○ ◐ ● ◑ ○

Call of the Wild

Coven or Solitary Ritual (Purple)
by Ivy

MAGICKAL INTENTION: To find your familiar.

TIME: Friday the Thirteenth, Waning Moon, Moon hour

TOOLS: One purple candle, Vision oil, Tiger incense, a red flannel mojo, a small found feather, an eye of newt (the center of a daisy, not the real eye of an animal), a naturally fallen cat's whisker, a tuft of dog's hair (from a dog's brush), a piece of a spiderweb, seven drops of salt water, a bowl, a quarter-cup of oats, corn, or seeds, a quarter-cup of raw hamburger, a quarter-cup of dried fruit, and a quarter-cup of raw vegetables.

INSTRUCTIONS: Anoint the candle with the Vision oil. Light the candle and the incense. In the mojo combine the feather, eye of newt, whisker, dog fur, web, and salt water. Tie the mojo shut and pass it in deosil motion through the incense smoke. Recite the incantation three times. In the bowl, combine the grain, meat, fruit, and veggies.

Take the bowl and the mojo outside, and place the bowl on the ground. Recite the incantation three times. Leave the bowl and keep the mojo with you. Return to this same place on the following day in the daylight hours and your familiar will appear to you.

INCANTATION:

> Creatures of the day and night,
> Slither, walk, fly, or crawl.
> Bring thy face into the light,
> Listen to my beck and call.
> Reveal to me the one that's right,
> Creature on which my eyes will fall.
> Do my bidding as my pet,
> Aid this Witch without regret.
> Creature with the power to see,
> Reveal the unknowable things that be.
> Show yourself and come to me,

Help me to sense what I cannot see.
Creatures of the day and night,
Come to me in the hours of light.
This is my will, So Mote It Be.

○ ◗ ● ◗ ○

The Banishment
of Beelzebub

Solitary or Coven Ritual (Black/Brown)
by Sister Moon

MAGICKAL INTENTION: To exorcise a demon from someone.

TIME: Friday the Thirteenth, Waning Moon, Saturn hour. This spell must be performed without the recipient's knowledge.

TOOLS: One black candle, Exorcism oil, Exorcism incense, a cup of fresh coffee grounds, a cup of sea salt, a piece of mandrake, a mortar and pestle, three found crow feathers, and a footprint of the person who needs the exorcism.

INSTRUCTIONS: Anoint the candle with the Exorcism oil. Light the candle and the incense. Place the coffee grounds, sea salt, and mandrake into the mortar and grind into small pieces. Stir the mixture widdershins with the three crow's feathers. Recite the incantation. Place the mixture into the footprint and place the three crow's feathers so they are upright in the print. The demon will be driven out by the full moon.

INCANTATION:

Widdershins stir the blackened bean,
Feather of crow with waxing sheen.
Remove the demon inside kept,
Of the one who made this step.
Mortar and pestle stir the salt,
Make possession come to halt.
Out you be demon of black,
Cease and desist this attack.
Turn and stir potion in reverse,
Unlock the holds of this curse.
Potion in print and feathers erect,
Beelzebub gone, I now protect.
So Mote It Be.

○ ◐ ● ◑ ○

Yesterday's Energy

Solitary Ritual (Purple)
by Queen of the Meadow

MAGICKAL INTENTION: To divine the history of an antique.

TIME: Friday the Thirteenth, Waning Moon, Moon hour

TOOLS: One purple candle, Psychic oil, Oracle incense, and your favorite antique.

INSTRUCTIONS: Anoint the candle with Psychic oil. Light the candle and the incense. Use your dominant hand rather than your power hand to divine your antique. Find the heart of the antique by feeling for its actual beat or pulse. Recite the incantation while your dominant hand is over the heart of the antique. Sit, touch the antique, lie down, or whatever you feel comfortable doing, and allow the memories to surface.

INCANTATION:

> I channel the spirit of the past,
> A memory awakened slow and fast.
> Bring forth the magick of second sight,
> Reveal the history upon this night.
> Soul retained in cloth and wood,
> Tears of joy, bad and good.
> Thirteenth Friday in its wane,
> Expose this picture within this frame.
> So Mote It Be.